Small Intarsia Projects You Can Make

by
Judy Gale Roberts
and
Jerry Booher

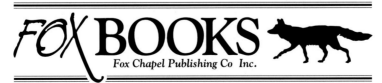

FOX BOOKS
Fox Chapel Publishing Co Inc.

PO Box 7948
Lancaster, PA   17604-7948

Publisher: Alan Giagnocavo
Project Editor: Ayleen Stellhorn
Electronic Specialist:Bob Altland, Altland Design
Photography: Curtis Doolan of Doolan, Langford Group, Lufkin, Texas
Cover Photography: Bob Polett, VMI Communications

ISBN #156523-062-0

To order your copy of this book,
please send check or money order
for cover price plus $2.50 to:
Fox Chapel Book Orders
Box 7948
Lancaster, PA 17604-7948

Try your favorite book supplier first!

Manufactured In China

Table of Contents

◈ *Foreword*

I first started doing Intarsia with my father, artist Pat Dudley Roberts, in the late 1970s. He always had a shop of sorts where he created everything from sculptures to large paintings for private collectors and commercial establishments. Our Intarsia projects at that time were large and roughly sanded with a low relief. I had fun mixing different shades of wood, then working with sanders to get a variety of effects. It was a very creative environment; there were no woodworking rules to limit us. In fact, when Jerry first came to our shop, he looked at our band saws and was amazed we could cut anything that would fit anything.

Jerry Booher and I began working together in the mid-1980s. We scaled down the size of the finished pieces and began exhibiting them at arts and craft shows. I showed Jerry how my father and I had made our wood murals. After studying the process, Jerry came up with some ideas and different approaches to get, as he said, "better results." I was a little reluctant to go along with him, after all, he was a newcomer to this and how could he come up with something better than my father and I. Finally I gave in and was glad I did. The total appearance of the projects changed. Everything was nicely sanded, more attention was paid to the small details.

After the first few arts and crafts shows, Jerry was inspired to find out if there was a name for this technique. He sent a letter along with photos to the National Woodcarvers Association and asked them if they could shine any light on the subject. We got a letter back and to my surprise there was a name for this method of woodworking. We looked in the Webster's Dictionary and there it was: Intarsia. I had mixed feelings: I was a little disappointed because I thought we had come up with this style of woodworking, but glad there was an official name. Indeed, our business changed quite a bit because of the name.

Here in this book, you'll find 13 small Intarsia projects specifically designed for the scroll-saw enthusiast. (With some modifications, they could also be cut out on a band saw.) These projects are free-form in nature, allowing them to be used for jewelry boxes, plates, furniture, cabinets and a number of other projects.

If you're new to Intarsia, you'll want to take a close look at the first several chapters. Chapter One covers wood selection for Intarsia projects. Chapter Two includes a pattern and step-by-step instructions and photographs for creating an Intarsia cat that also functions as a pin cushion. Chapter Three, which covers how to make a large-mouth bass, also includes a pattern and step-by-step instructions and photographs. The remainder of the chapters include a pattern for each project and accompanying tips to help you get started.

We hope that the color photos and step-by-step instructions will prove beneficial and that you enjoy Intarsia as much as we do!

> Before you get started, we want to urge you to develop good safety practices any time you are using any type of woodworking machinery or hand tools, as well as using good common sense when using finishes of any kind. Please make safety glasses and hearing protection standard procedure when using any type of machinery. Be sure to read and follow the manufacturers recommendations for power tool safety, as well as to read and follow the safety recommendations for the use of finishes (good ventilation and lots of it!).

Chapter One
Wood Selection

◈ Wood Selection

Photo 1:1

Any type of wood will work for Intarsia projects. The most important aspects of the wood you choose are color and grain patterns. You may choose to use walnut or red cedar for dark wood, maybe pecan for a medium color, and maple or birch for a light shade.

Photo 1:1 on the opposite page shows eight pieces of wood. Most of the wood I use, and most of the blocks shown here, is western red cedar. I prefer to use western red cedar because of the wide variety of colors and grain patterns produced by the tree. There are two types of red cedar: Western red cedar, which comes in a wide variety of colors, and red aromatic cedar, which is mostly red-white with some purple. Both are easy to work and perfect for wall-hanging projects that don't get the abuse that furniture projects do. For the white color in my projects, I use either white pine, basswood or aspen. The white wood pictured here is basswood. Like western red cedar, basswood also has its variances and can range in color from a very tan to an almost pure white.

I use letter codes on the patterns in this book to indicate the color of the wood to use in making these Intarsia projects. Look closely at the samples of wood in Photo 1:1; they will give you an idea of the different shades of wood used in the projects.

From left to right, the first piece of wood would be referred to with a W for white wood, the second, L for a light shade of wood, the third, M for a medium shade of wood, and the fourth, ML for a medium-light shade of wood. The first sample on the lower row would be labeled with a MD for a medium-dark shade of wood, the second is another MD, the third is D for a dark shade of wood, and the final sample on the lower row is also a D for yet a darker shade or wood.

We applied a clear finish to the lower half

of each block to show you what the wood will look like once a clear finish is applied. The wood becomes at least one shade darker when a clear finish is applied. White wood, such as basswood, pine or aspen, is the least affected by the finish. In addition to making the wood look darker and richer in color, the finish will also bring out the grain.

Wood for Intarsia projects can be found at your local lumber yard. I buy my Western red cedar at several different lumber yards so that I can find a variety of colors. Lumber yards sell cedar in a number of widths from 1" x 2" boards to 1" x 12" boards. I have found that the darker shades of cedar are harder to find. I have better luck looking through the cedar fence picket pile. Even the 1" x 4" section may have more dark cedar than the 1" x 12" section. For these smaller Intarsia projects, the 1" x 6" fence pickets have ample width and provide an inexpensive wood to use.

Photo 1:2

Sometimes with cedar, I am able to find the sap wood, which is often very white. On a living tree, the sap wood is located next to the bark. Sap flows through this wood and delivers nutrients to the tree. At the lumber yard, you can find sap wood on the outside edges of cedar boards. The white color of sap wood is usually limited to about two inches wide.

Photo 1:3

When choosing which boards to buy, I look for color first, then I take a closer look to see what the grains are doing. One of the most intriguing parts of choosing wood for Intarsia is finding not only a color, but a grain pattern that can make a project come to life. I rarely buy the "knot-free" lumber. So many times, you will find really unusual grain patterns around a knot. Since we are working with many small parts, it is easy to work around the knots and other natural occurrences in the wood. Sometimes, I even incorporate the knot into the project; other times I discard it if the knot is too dark and tends to draw too much attention away from the main subject matter.

Photo 1:4

I also look for wood that may have some streaks going through it. These pieces make great wood for sunsets, water and even rose petals (as you will see on the rose jewelry box design on page 55).

I also buy straight-grained lumber so that on each project I have a balance of straight grains and unusual grains. Too many exotic grain patterns can get monotonous.

I stash away many prize boards that are waiting for just the "right project." Sometimes the wood will inspire the pattern. I now find myself studying wood everywhere and enjoying its natural beauty.

After making your wood selections, make sure the wood is dry. If you use wet wood for Intarsia projects, the parts will shrink as the wood dries, leaving gaps between the pieces.

Photo 1:1 Wood comes in a wide variety of colors and grain patterns. These eight wood samples show the color of the unfinished wood and the finished wood.

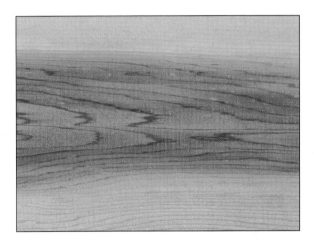

Photo 1:2 Though it is hard to find, red cedar sap wood can be used as white-colored wood in place of the more common basswood, pine or aspen.

Photo 1:3 Knots in wood often force the grain of the wood to form interesting and unusual patterns that are beautiful when incorporated into Intarsia projects.

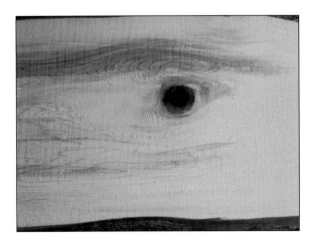

Photo 1:4 Streaks of color going through pieces of wood are perfect for creating sunsets and water.

You will need one 1/8" dowel for the eyes.

Make your photo copies of the pattern at 100%.

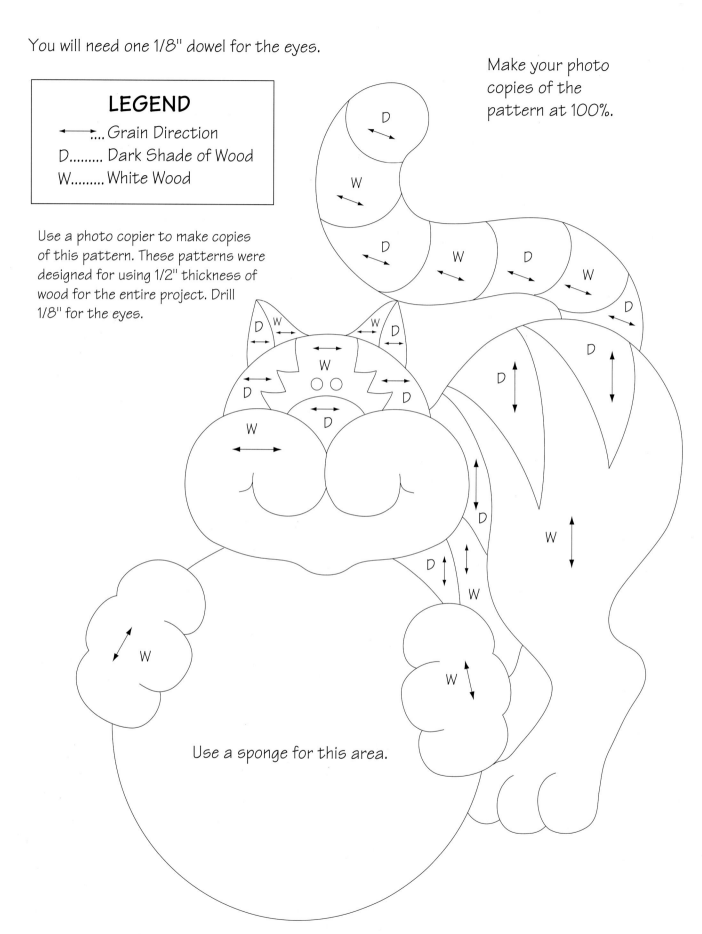

LEGEND

←——→ .... Grain Direction
D......... Dark Shade of Wood
W......... White Wood

Use a photo copier to make copies of this pattern. These patterns were designed for using 1/2" thickness of wood for the entire project. Drill 1/8" for the eyes.

Use a sponge for this area.

For detailed instructions for making this project, read the chapter on the Pin Cushion Cat.

Chapter Two
Pin Cushion Cat

STEP ONE:
LAYING OUT THE PATTERN

Photo 1:1

Before you begin, note the grain directions, shown with an arrow, and the color suggestions, shown with a letter, on each segment of the pattern. Areas where the grain directions are going the same way, often can be stack-cut. (Stack cutting refers to cutting two different-colored pieces of wood at the same time and swapping the pieces to create a multi-colored section. But, I'll go more into depth about stack cutting in Photos 1:4 and 1:5.) Decide at this time which sections can be stack-cut.

On this pattern of a pin cushion cat, there are three sections that can be stack cut: the tail section, the hind leg section and the head section. In other words, we'll be cutting the entire tail, hind leg and head out of light and dark wood at the same time. If you want to have two cats when you are finished sawing, then you will want to stack-cut the paws also.

For these small projects I chose to use wood that is 1/2" thick. Smaller sized projects look very dimensional using only 1/2" thick material. On larger projects, I will use up to 2"–thick material to give it the depth needed to keep it from looking flat.

Photo 1:2

Cut the pattern into sections. Before you do this step, you'll need to make at least five copies of the cat pattern. You'll need at least this many copies because cutting out the different sections makes the remainder of the pattern unusable for the adjoining sections. So, from one copy, cut the tail; from a second, cut the hind leg section; from a third, cut the head section; and from a fourth, cut the paws. Be sure to leave some extra space on the outside of the lines.

It is a good habit to number the parts. This project does not have that many parts, but some in the future may. I keep one pattern as a master and number the parts on it, then put those same numbers on the parts to be cut out.

Photo 1:3

Before adhering the pattern to the wood, study the wood for grain patterns. I always mark interesting sections first, because once you attach the pattern, it will be hard to see the grain through the opaque paper.

Use some repositioning spray adhesive to apply the pattern to the wood. To adhere the pattern to the wood, spray the adhesive on the back side of the paper pattern. If my wood is to be stack-cut, I generally put the pattern on the lighter of the two woods. Here, I have applied the pattern sections to the white wood.

After the pattern is in place, I use a scroll saw to cut around the section, leaving about a 1/2" border. Then I trace the outline of the white section onto the dark wood.

Note the arrows marked on some of the pattern edges. These arrows indicate the outside edges and edges that don't touch other parts of the cat. These edges are not as critical as others in the cutting stage because they don't have to fit against other adjoining pieces. You can relax a little while cutting these areas.

Photo 1:4

After cutting the dark section, I use double-sided carpet tape to stick the two sections together. The tape generally comes in 1 1/2" to 2" widths. I cut the tape into 1/4" strips. Sometimes the tape, when used in its original width, is so aggressive that it is almost impossible to separate the sections after cutting. It is best to test your tape to determine how aggressive it is.

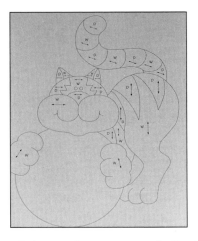

Photo 1:1 *Before you begin to cut out the Pin Cushion Cat, study the pattern carefully and note the arrows indicating grain direction and the letters suggesting wood color.*

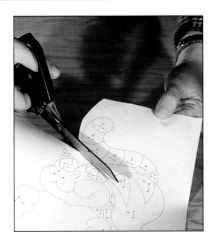

Photo 1:2 *Make several copies of your pattern before cutting out the sections. You'll need one copy for each section.*

Photo 1:3 *Glue the pattern to the wood with an adhesive spray. Cut out the sections leaving a ¹/₂″ border around the edge. Trace the shape onto the dark wood.*

Photo 1:4 *Cut the dark wood to shape and apply double-sided carpet tape to the wood.*

Photo 1:5 *Peel the backing away from the tape and stick both sections together. Both pieces of wood will be cut at once. This is known as stack-cutting.*

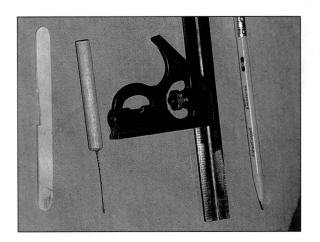

Photo 2:1 *A popsicle stick, a broken scroll saw blade, a square measure, a pencil and a sanding block (not shown here) are several tools that aid in making Intarsia projects.*

Photo 1:5
Be sure to put the tape in areas that will hold the parts together, even after cutting some of the sections apart. In this photo I am using an exacto knife to help peel the paper off the carpet tape.

STEP TWO
USING A SCROLL SAW

The methods of sawing covered in this book are for the scroll saw, although this in no way implies that one must use a scroll saw. If you plan to use a band saw, a $1/16"$ blade should allow you to make all the necessary cuts (although we have not tried using a band saw for these projects). Using a band saw will almost rule out the stack-cutting technique because of the blade's wide kerf (blade width).

I will assume that readers making these Intarsia projects have good, basic scroll saw skills. If you are just learning how to use a scroll saw, I would suggest that you obtain one or more of the following scroll saw books to familiarize yourself with the different techniques: *Learning to Use the Scroll Saw*, by Joanne Lockwood (She also has a companion video for this book which is sold separately.); *Scroll Saw Basics* and *The Scroll Saw Book*, both by Patrick Spielman.

In addition to reading the books mentioned above, you need to practice, practice, practice. There is no substitute for a large pile of wood, plenty of sharp blades and hours upon hours of practical scroll sawing.

The blade you choose to be your favorite is a personal thing. I have talked to countless people who use scroll saws, and it seems that we all have our favorite blade. Although just one blade type will not be adequate for all types of sawing, it seems that we all return to our favorite. My personal choice is a #2 regular-tooth blade. Some people seem to think that this blade is a little small for most applications, but it has worked well for me. I use a #2 exclusively for these Intarsia projects, except in areas that call for a vein to be cut. In those cases I used a larger (wider) blade to give more definition to the cut.

Scroll saw set up
When sitting down for a session, I check my scroll saw machine for squareness (in case I or someone else has tilted the table since the last time I used it and did not put it back square with the blade).

I start by checking the blade's squareness to the table with a small square. The blade and the table should be at right, or 90 degree, angles. I then make a cut across a piece of $3/4"$ to $1"$ thick stock and check that cut for squareness. Should the new cut across the piece of wood be "out of square," I make another cut the same way and check that one, too. Be sure to remove any burr on the bottom of the wood before starting the cut. Burr left on the wood could cause the block of wood to rock or sit at an angle and will give you an out-of-square cut even if your blade is square.

If you are convinced that the blade is not square with the table, now is the time to make an adjustment to the table to correct the problem. After any adjustment to the table, make another test cut to check for squareness. Repeat the steps above until you are satisfied with the squareness. Just remember to make sure that your test piece of wood is flat on the bottom and any burr has also been removed. Once I am satisfied that the saw is cutting square, I then proceed with my project.

Although I try to make every cut square, I have found that it is almost impossible to maintain squareness at all times because of the burr being created on the bottom side of the wood. I have, however, found a happy medium for my cutting. You will also find a

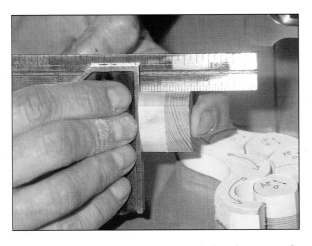

Photo 2:2 *Use a small square to check that the cuts made by the saw are at right angles.*

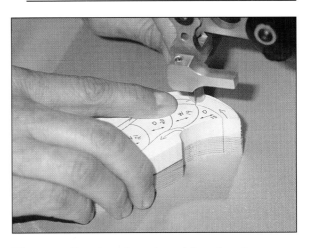

Photo 2:3 *Cut along the outline of the tail section.*

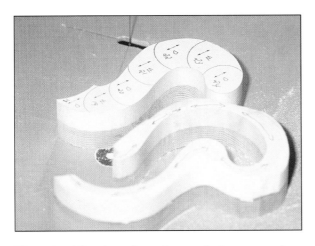

Photo 2:4 *This photo shows the completely cut out tail and the drop off section. Do not throw away the drop off section yet.*

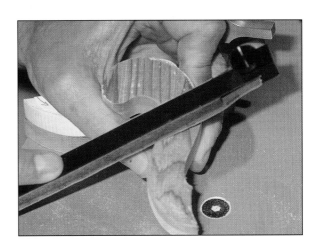

Photo 2:5 *Before making another cut, and after every subsequent cut, remove the burr from the bottom of the wood so the piece sits flat on the saw table.*

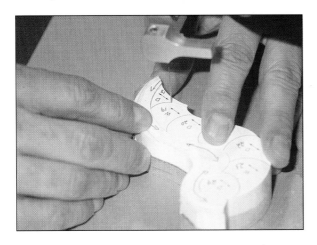

Photo 2:6 *Use the drop off piece to protect your fingers as you make the cuts that form the tail stripes.*

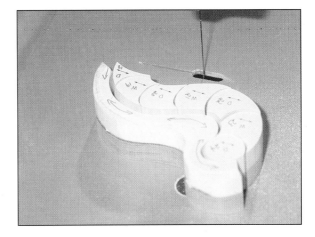

Photo 2:7 *Here, the tail stripes have been separated.*

happy medium that you can live with. Cuts that are out-of-square can also be caused by operator error—in fact that is my biggest problem. Too much cutting pressure or not feeding the wood directly into the face of the blade are my biggest reasons for cuts that are not square.

Photo 2:1

Shown here are tools that I have close at hand while working with my scroll saw.

The first tool on the left is a wooden popsicle stick. I have tapered the rounded ends of the stick and use it to hold down loose edges of my paper pattern. At times the pattern will have a tendency to flap a little if the adhesive is a little light, so I use the stick to hold down the flapping pattern instead of using my finger.

The second tool is a piece of a scroll saw blade that I have glued into the end of a dowel. I use this as a "push rod" when doing fret work. It helps me to remove the inside dropout piece.

The third tool is a 6" square. I use this square to check my wooden pieces for squareness. The square, along with a sander (not shown here), is one of the most important tools I use when cutting.

Last, but not least, is a pencil. It is important to mark the wood with a pencil; ink or marker can sink into the wood and show through on your final project.

I also have a sanding block on my table. More recently, I have been using a flat Intarsia Detail Sander (not shown here). I use this tool to remove the burr on the bottom side of the work piece, allowing the wood to sit flat on the table.

Photo 2:2

In this photo, I am using my small square to check a part for squareness. You can see by the two different colors of wood that this piece has been stack-cut. Stack cutting is the way to go for these miniatures, providing your machine cuts well and maintains a reasonable amount of squareness. Remember that the stock thickness is $1/2$", and we are going to cut two thickness. This will make the material 1" thick. It really does not matter which part you start cutting first, however, I usually start with the easiest one. This allows me to get into the swing of things.

Photo 2:3

The first cut of the cat's tail is made at the end of the tail where the tail meets the body. This area has to fit next to an adjoining part, so pay close attention to the saw cuts. Saw with the middle of the blade on the middle of the line. Next, I cut the outline of the tail. Because the outline of the tail does not fit next to any other piece, precise cutting is not mandatory.

Photo 2:4

In this photo, you can see the sawed-out tail and the drop-off piece. Do not throw the drop-off piece away yet; we will use half of it as a back-up when cutting the stripes.

Photo 2:5

Here, I am sanding the burr away from the backside of the tail. It is important to remove the burr prior to cutting the stripes so that the tail piece lays flat on the table. Also shown is the Intarsia Detail Sander mentioned earlier.

Photo 2:6

After de-burring the backside of the tail, I carefully cut out the stripes. Look closely and you'll see that I am using part of the drop-off piece from Photo 2:4 to cut the stripes. This back-up block helps to protect your hands as you make the cuts for the tail stripes.

Photo 2:8 *The pattern for the head section has been applied to the wood. Light wood and dark wood are taped together for a stack cut.*

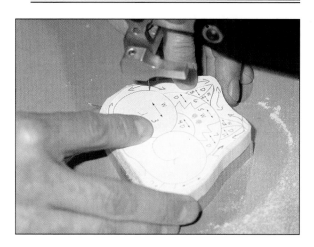

Photo 2:9 *Cut the head section. Be careful to follow the lines exactly on the right side where the cat's head meets the body.*

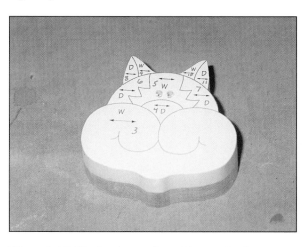

Photo 2:10 *The head, complete with ears, has been cut out and is now ready to be separated into parts.*

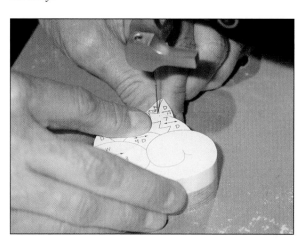

Photo 2:11 *It takes three cuts to separate the ear parts. The first cut is made along the bottom left of the right ear.*

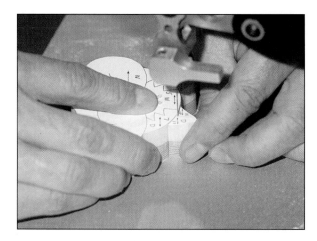

Photo 2:12 *The second cut follows the vertical line down the center of the ear.*

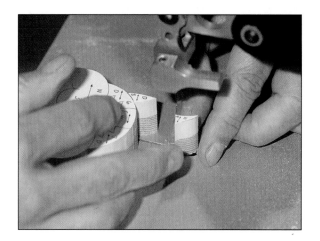

Photo 2:13 *The two cuts performed in Photos 2:11 and 2:12 result in the first part of the ear to be separated from the head.*

Photo 2:7

Here you can see the tail stripes once they have been cut apart. The back-up block that I used to protect my fingers is shown on the left. It can now be thrown away.

Cutting the back leg section

Next, I cut the back leg section and then the front paws. These steps are not shown here, as the instructions are similar to cutting the cat's tail. However, there are several points you'll want to keep in mind.

When cutting the back leg section, I first cut all the way around the section on the pattern outline. I did not make the cuts into the toes at this time. After the outline is cut, I then cut the stripes away from the back. Next, I cut out the three sections between the cheeks and the front paw. Remember to remove the burr on the bottom of the section after each cut. Again, I did not make the cuts for the toes yet; that step will come later. I leave the parts taped together until I am finished with all the cutting.

The next sections to be cut are the front paws. Again, I only cut the outline of the paws and did not cut the toes yet.

Photo 2:8

The outline of the head section is ready to be cut. Note that the eyes were drilled before any cutting is done. I am stack-cutting the head section from two different pieces of wood. When the head is completely cut out, I'll be able to mix and match light and dark pieces.

Photo 2:9

The entry cut is made at the top of the right ear to the base of the ear and then over the forehead and the left ear. The cut continues on, all away around the outer perimeter of the head. Make sure your cuts are precise on the right edges of the cat's head. These edges will need to fit next to adjoining pieces. The other edges, those that do not meet adjoining pieces, do not need to be cut as precisely.

Photo 2:10

This photo shows the head section of the cat completely cut out. I am now ready to cut the head section into parts.

Photo 2:11

The ears are the first parts to be cut away from the head section. I make the first cut along the left side of right ear where the head meets the ear. I continue to cut until just past the vertical line that separates the ear into two parts. When I reach this point, I stop cutting and back out of the cut.

Photo 2:12

Here, I am making the second cut to the right ear. I cut from the tip of the ear down to the first cut, until this small ear part drops off.

Photo 2:13

The first part of the ear is completely cut away from the head section. I now go back to where the first cut stopped and continue around the head until the other part of this ear is cut off. I then move on to the next ear, cutting it the same way.

Photo 2:14

After the ears have been cut off, the forehead/nose section is then cut away from the cheeks. I do not cut the smile at this point.

Photo 2:15

After I have removed the burr from the back side of the forehead/nose section, I can cut out the zig-zag sections on the outside of the head. Quick turns are necessary to cut out this section. After I finish the zig-zag sections, I cut away the nose.

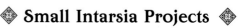

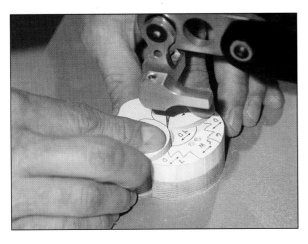

Photo 2:14 *This photo shows the author cutting the fore-head and nose sections.*

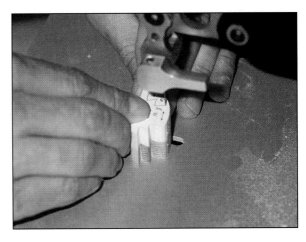

Photo 2:15 *The zig-zag cuts on the outer sides of the head require quick turns.*

Photo 2:16 *To make the cut for the mouth, follow along the lines to the end of the smile.*

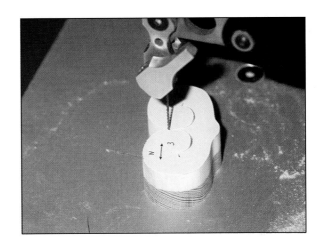

Photo 2:17 *To cut the little curves at the ends of the cat's smile, first back the saw into the lines you cut previously...*

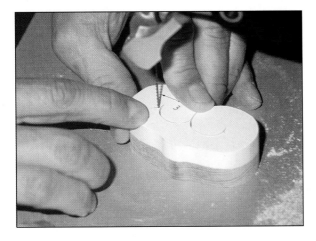

Photo 2:18 *then cut the small curved lines.*

Photo 3:1 *Stack cutting the pieces for the cat gives us two versions of the same project with different color combinations. Number the back of all the parts before proceeding.*

Photo 2:16

After all the parts have been cut, I change from a #2 blade to a #9 blade. The #9 blade has a wider kerf (blade width) and works well for cutting the smile. Note in this photo that both sides of the smile were cut only to the ends of the smile. You won't be able to cut the little curves at the end of the smile at this point. To cut that little curve, I back the blade out of the smile and then into the smile to the end and then cut the little curve. After both sides of the smile have been cut, I cut the toes and back foot lines using the same blade.

Photo 2:17

In this photo, you can see how the blade is backed into the initial cuts of the cat's smile.

Photo 2:18

Here, the blade has been fed all the way to the end of the smile. I am now preparing to make the final cut.

STEP THREE
SHAPING THE CAT

Photo 3:1

After all the parts are cut out, I carefully take apart the two sections. I remove any burr and number the back of each part. I stack cut all the parts so as you can see the two complete cats, with opposite markings.

Photo 3:2

I cut a "template" for the ball section out of a scrap piece of cedar. I used spray adhesive to apply the pattern to the wood. This will help keep the parts together while shaping and will be used for some of the other steps in this project.

This is a good time to check the overall fit of the cat. Carefully mark and trim areas that need some reworking. The cat looks very flat

at this time; everything is 1/2" thick. I start to shape the pieces by sanding those that would be the farthest from the viewer. By lowering these parts it makes the unsanded parts stand out more.

Photo 3:3

For sanding work, I use a pneumatic drum sander that has two drums. There are a number of different-sized drums available. I like to have one drum fitted with 100-grit paper and the other with a well-worn 120-grit. I use the 100-grit paper to rough-in the part, and the 120-grit to clean up the part. I try to sand with the grain whenever possible. For these small projects the smaller drums are easier to use. You'll have less of a chance to sand your fingers. (For more information on pneumatic sanders, see the buyers guide on page 28.) You can also use disc and belt sanders to shape the parts. When I first started doing Intarsia, I did not have drum sanders and used the disc and belt sanders with good results.

Photo 3:4

This photo shows a very reasonably priced sander called the Flex Sander. It has a foam pad that works like the pneumatic sanders. (See the buyers guide for details.) The little drum sanders you see in many of the woodworking catalogs will also work well. Many of the drums available have a hard rubber drum with the sanding sleeve wrapped around it. The pneumatic and the Flex Sander have some give to them. With some pressure you can squeeze the softer drums, which makes them easier to use for softly rounding parts.

Photo 3:5

This project has many areas that can be sanded together as if they were one piece of wood. These areas are the tail section, the hind leg,

Photo 3:2 *Cutting a wooden template for the ball, which will actually be created from a sponge later, helps to keep the pieces in place for now.*

Photo 3:3 *This pneumatic drum sander has two drums. The drum sander will be used to shape and round the parts of the cat.*

Photo 3:4 *The Flex Sander, another type of sander, works similarly to the pneumatic drum sander. Both can be used for Intarsia projects.*

Photo 3:5 *A sanding shim, which will be used to hold the pieces together during sanding, was cut according to the pattern.*

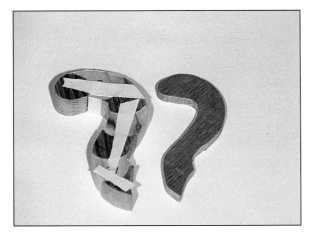

Photo 3:6 *The tail, the hind leg and the upper face can all be sanded as one piece. You'll need to cut a shim for each of these areas.*

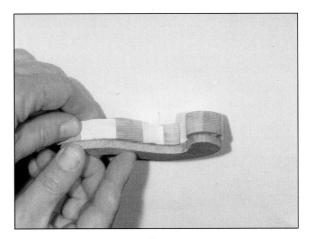

Photo 3:7 *Attach the shim to the sections using double-sided tape.*

and the upper face section. I cut a sanding shim, using the pattern or the actual parts as a guide. A sanding shim is simply a temporary backing to which the parts are taped. Use a piece of scrap plywood and either use the pattern or trace around the parts to get an outline of the project. I use a saw to cut it out, and then I use double-sided tape to hold the pieces together on the backing while I sand them.

Photo 3:6

As mentioned above, we will be lowering pieces. I start with the parts that would be farthest away from the viewer, as if looking at a three-dimensional model. Where the cat's tail joins its body is the farthest away, so I sand it first. I prepare the tail section by placing it upside down and putting strips of double-sided tape on the back to keep all the parts together.

I then sand the remaining parts in this order: the hind leg section, the ears, the upper face area, the paws and finally the smile section of the face, marking with a pencil each step of the way. After each section is sanded, use a pencil to mark the adjoining parts. These marks will act as a guide for sanding the next piece. You do not want to sand below the pencil lines.

Photo 3:7

After peeling the backing off the tape, I attach the sanding shim to the tail section.

Photo 3:8

First, I rough-in the tail section. I tapered the tail down to about 1/4" where it joins the body. I hold on to the end of the tail, which will remain thick and easy to hold on to. After I get the desired taper, I round the outside edges as much as possible with the sander to create a smooth, flowing edge.

Photo 3:9

Because of the sharp curl in the tail I had to do some hand sanding to get the rounded look all the way around the tail. To get into the sharp curve, a file or the Intarsia Detail Sander, which has a pad under the sanding strip, or even a rounded exacto blade can remove material where needed. It is important to remember to just rough-in the project at this point. You may need to re-sand some areas later.

Photo 3:10

After you are satisfied with the tail, disassemble it from the backing and place the parts where they belong on the master pattern. I use the master pattern (the one we numbered at the beginning) to work off of, that way I can see where the tail is supposed to join the body.

Photo 3:11

With a pencil, I mark the height of the tail where it joins the body. When you sand the body section, this marked area will give you an indication of when to stop sanding. You do not want to sand the hind leg area lower than the tail.

Photo 3:12

Next, prepare the hind leg section for sanding. Use the double-sided tape to hold the pieces to the sanding shim. Note the pencil line showing where the tail joins the body.

Photo 3:13

You will want to lower the area that joins the head. I sanded the pieces that touch the face and the one paw down to about 1/4" thick, leaving the area around the tail thicker. Note that I did not sand below the pencil line.

Photo 3:14

Once I've sanded the sections so they have a

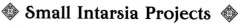

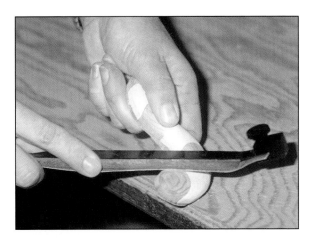

Photo 3:8 *Using the drum sander, rough-in the tail section. The edges of the tail should taper down to about ¹/4″ where it joins the body.*

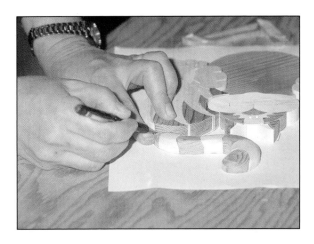

Photo 3:9 *Use an Intarsia Detail Sander to rough-in the areas around the sharp curve in the cat's tail.*

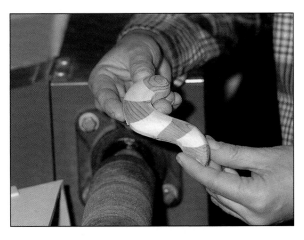

Photo 3:10 *Once you are satisfied with the sanding, remove the pieces from the shim and place them in their correct positions on the master pattern.*

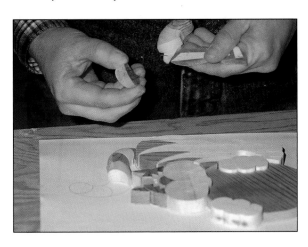

Photo 3:11 *Use a pencil to mark the height of the tail on the body where the tail joins it. This mark will act as a guide when sanding the body.*

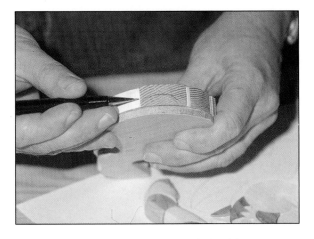

Photo 3:12 *Mount the pieces from the hind leg section on a sanding shim. Note the pencil mark added in Photo 3:11.*

Photo 3:13 *Sand the pieces that touch the face and the one paw down to about ¹/4″. Leave the area around the tail thicker.*

nice, flowing taper, I take the hind leg portion off the backing. With the hind leg section removed, I can to sand the cat's stomach area lower than the leg without sanding the leg.

Photo 3:15

Now I can carefully taper the stomach portion down toward the outside edge. Be sure to sand the stomach section only. At this point, you do not want to sand into the back area where the stripes are located.

Photo 3:16

Put the leg section back in place to see if there is enough of a stair step between the parts. I like to have at least 1/8" step up to the leg section. This helps to give more definition to the hind leg and gives more dimension to the leg. If there is not enough of the stomach portion sanded off, keep sanding until you get the desired thickness. You can disassemble the parts from the shim at this time.

Photo 3:17

I do some detail sanding on the toes. I like to round them almost as if they were little grapes. There are a number of techniques to accomplish this. I use the Wonder Wheel which is handy for light carving and other types of detail work.

Photo 3:18

The Wonder Wheel carves and burns the wood at the same time. To get into tight areas, I use the corner of the wheel, which works great on small areas like those between the toes.

Photo 3:19

You could also use an exacto knife to remove the wood between the toes. Either way, you will still need to do some hand-sanding to smooth out the toes.

Photo 3:20

The Intarsia Detail Sander blends these areas with ease. Depending on the pressure used, you can take off more or less wood. If you want to remove a lot of material you can use a rougher grit paper.

Photo 3:21

Mark with your pencil the area where the body joins the head and paws. Next, sand the ears down to about 1/4" or less. After sanding the ears, mark where they join the head.

Photo 3:22

Next, I sand the upper head section using the double-sided tape and a sanding shim. When you sand the head, remember to watch for those pencil guidelines. Don't sand below the lines.

Photo 3:23

Lower the upper head section to about 3/8", rounding it toward the back where the ears are located.

Photo 3:24

Always watch for your pencil lines while you are sanding. Sometimes, I get carried away and sand off too much. This is an easy mistake to make when you're rounding the head. If you round off too much you can go back and sand some more off the ears.

Photo 3:25

After shaping the head, mark the adjoining pieces with your pencil. Using your pencil line as a guide, sand the nose, leaving it a little thicker than the upper head section. Then mark the nose section where it joins the upper smile section.

Photo 3:26

Note the pencil lines I have drawn here.

Photo 3:14 *To sand the stomach area of the cat without sanding the leg, remove the hind leg section from the sanding shim.*

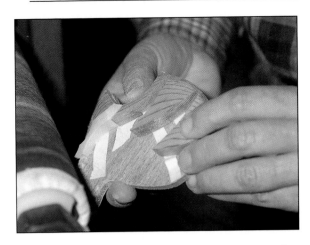

Photo 3:15 *Taper the stomach down toward the outside edge.*

Photo 3:16 *Reassemble the pieces to check the "stair step" between the stomach and the leg and mark the height with a pencil. Disassemble the pieces.*

Photo 3:17 *Use a Wonder Wheel to detail-sand the toes. Here, I am rounding them like little grapes.*

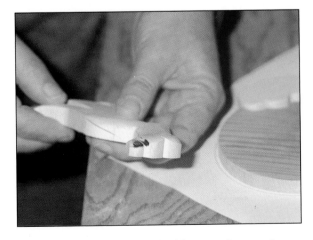

Photo 3:18 *The Wonder Wheel burns and carves the wood at the same time.*

Photo 3:19 *Use an exacto knife to remove the wood between the toes. Hand-sand the toes once the wood has been removed.*

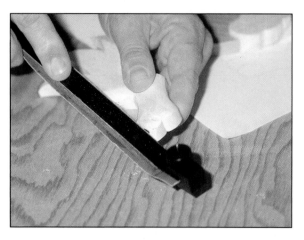

Photo 3:20 *Use an Intarsia Detail Sander to blend the toes into the surrounding area.*

Photo 3:21 *Use a pencil to mark the height of the body where it joins the head. Sand the ears down to about ¹/4" or less. Mark their height as well.*

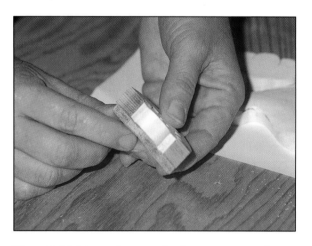

Photo 3:22 *Mount the upper head section to a sanding shim with double-sided tape.*

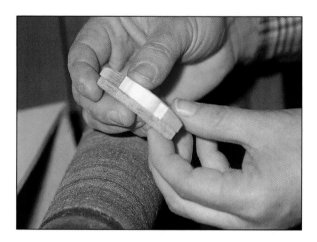

Photo 3:23 *Round the upper head section back toward the ears. Lower it to about 3/8".*

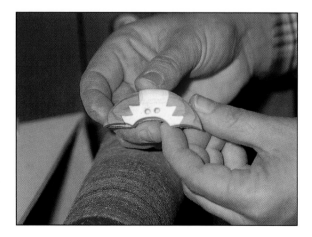

Photo 3:24 *Follow your pencil guides as you sand, being careful not to remove too much wood.*

Photo 3:25 *Sand the nose. Leave it a little thicker than the upper head section.*

Photo 3:26 *These pencil lines show how far down to sand this section of the head.*

Photo 3: 27 *Rough-in the smile section and then hand-sand it to give it some detail.*

Photo 3:28 *To make the cheeks look more puffy, use an exacto knife to remove wood below the cat's smile.*

Photo 3:29 *Removing about ¹/16″ makes the upper cheeks the thickest part of the face.*

Photo 3:30 *Hand-sand the area under the smile to achieve a smooth surface and eliminate any "step" between the areas.*

Photo 3:31 *This photo shows nicely shaped cheeks. However, the veining lines of the smile still need some work.*

When I shape this part, I do not want to sand below these lines. Because the cheek sections are closest to the viewer, I want them to be the thickest parts of the face. If I sand below the guide lines, I will need to go back and re-sand the head section so that it is thinner than the cheek.

Photo 3:27

First, I rough-in the smile section on the sander. I take off some wood under the smile on the chin, but not much. I remove just enough to keep it from looking flat. I also round the outside edges. Then it's back to putting some detail in by hand around the smile to give it some definition.

Photo 3:28

I want to lower the part under the smile to make the checks more puffy-looking. I found it easiest to just use the rounded exacto knife to carve this.

Photo 3:29

Remove enough wood from the cheeks (about 1/16" or more) to make the upper cheeks the thickest part.

Photo 3:30

Then, as always, after removing wood, the cheeks will need some hand-sanding. I like to round the upper check section down toward the area carved, so there is not a sharp "step-down."

Photo 3:31

The smile section has been carved and sanded to the shape I want, but the lines defining the smile look pretty bad.

Photo 3:32

The Intarsia Bow Sander works great for getting to those hard to reach areas and veining lines like those on the smile. It works just like its name implies. It has a strip of sandpaper stretched with clamps at either end of the bow to keep it in place. You can also fold a piece of sand paper to get in those areas.

Photo 3:33

The smile shows up much better once the area has been cleaned up.

Photo 3:34

I then rough-in the paws on the sander. I don't remove a lot of wood here; mostly the paws are just rounded. Watch out for the pencil lines where the one paw joins the body.

Photo 3:35

I carve the toes on the paws using the same techniques that I used on the hind leg toes. Do both paws the same way, watching out for the pencil line on the right paw. When you are satisfied with the cat's shape go ahead and finish-sand the entire project. Sometimes it may help to tape the sections back to the sanding shim to make it easier to hand-sand the project. By "finish-sand," I mean to go back and sand all the pieces, sanding with the grain direction. I do a lot of this by hand, however, if there are deep scratches, I will use the sander. I work my way from 120-grit paper up to about 220-grit paper. The higher the number, the finer the grit on the sand paper and the smoother the surface of your project will be.

Photo 3:36

To create the eyes, I used a 1/8" dowel. I cut a section about 1 1/2" long and slightly rounded both ends. I used the Wonder Wheel to burn and round the dowel at the same time. You could use a wood burner or stain to darken the eyes. If you can locate a 1/8" walnut dowel, there will be no need to darken it for the eyes.

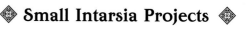

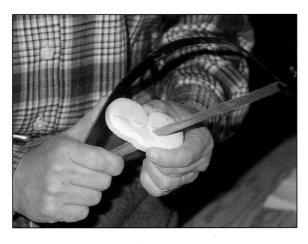

Photo 3:32 *Use an Intarsia Bow Sander or a piece of folded sand paper to sand the smile.*

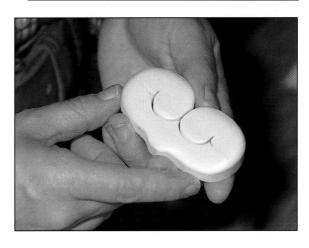

Photo 3:33 *The smile shows up much better once it has been sanded.*

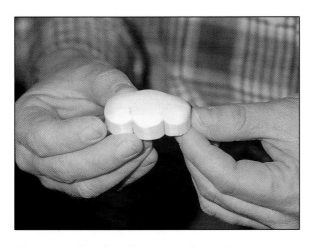

Photo 3:34 *Rough-in the paws on the sander.*

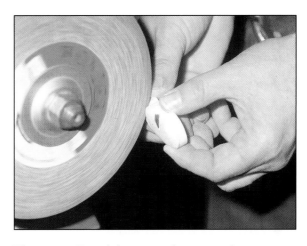

Photo 3:35 *Round the toes on the paws in the same manner as the toes on the hind legs were rounded. Finish-sand the entire project.*

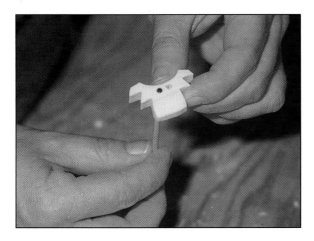

Photo 3:36 *Use a 1/8" dowel for the eyes and round them with a Wonder Wheel or an exacto knife. Darken them with a wood burner or stain.*

Photo 3:37 *Insert the dowel into the eye from the back of the face. Mark the dowel with a pencil and cut the dowel flush with the piece.*

Photo 3:3

I then put the dowel in the pre-drilled hole for the eye and mark the dowel from the backside of the head. I like to have the eyes almost flush with the head to keep the cat from looking "bug-eyed."

Photo 3:38

After both dowels are cut, I glue them in. I put the glue in from the back side. Then I put the dowels in from the front. I also use a piece of masking tape to keep the glue from oozing out the back side.

Photo 3:39

The last step is to lightly sand the edges of all the parts to knock off the sharp corners and to erase any remaining pencil marks. I put the ball template in place and check the project to make sure the shaping is what I want before I proceed.

STEP FOUR
CUTTING AND SHAPING
THE PIN CUSHION

Photo 4:1

I found a rather firm, tight-holed sponge to make the pin cushion. Use some spray adhesive to apply the pin cushion portion of the pattern (the ball between the cat's paws) to some chip board (a thin cardboard, like on the back of note pads). Then spray adhesive on the back of the chip board and stick it on top of the sponge. Attaching the sponge to the stiff chip board will make the sponge easier to cut. Cut the sponge with the scroll saw or a band saw. You will find that this step is easier with a band saw. Use caution when cutting this sponge as it cuts very easily, making it hard to control the saw blade. I would suggest taking several test cuts before starting to cut the actual sponge.

Photo 4:2

Use scissors to trim the sponge in a ball shape.

Photo 4:3

The sponge I used was firm enough to sand on the sander. I used the template that I cut out earlier and placed it behind the sponge to keep the sponge flat while I sand it. If you cannot find a firm sponge, you can trim it just with the scissors. Do not worry about making it perfectly round—maybe the cat tore it up! I used a blue spray paint to make the sponge a more pleasing color.

STEP FIVE
FINISHING THE PIN CUSHION

Photo 5:1

After all the parts have been sanded, checked for scratches, de-burred and dusted off, it is time to put a clear finish on the parts. I put the finish on before I glued the pieces down. It is easier to get a nice finish this way. Also, glue that has been dropped on a piece is easier to wipe off of a finished piece. You'll also avoid the light spots that occur when you apply finish over unseen (until now) glue residue. I use Bartley Wiping Gel, a polyurethane in a gel base. I've found it is one of the easiest finishes with which to get professional results. (See the buyers guide for more information.) There is no need for sanding between coats. I apply three coats, waiting at least four hours before applying each subsequent coat.

Once the clear finish has been applied to all the pieces, I glue some of the stripes together. I started with those on the tail, back and face. I use just a dot of hot glue, placed low in the seam, to keep the glue from squeezing up between the parts. When using the hot glue, you will need to move quickly. Have your parts lined up and ready to go.

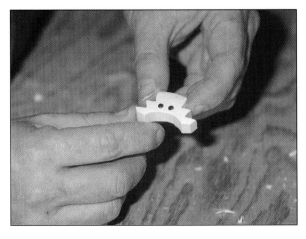

Photo 3:38 *Glue the dowels into the eye holes.*

Photo 3:39 *Lightly sand the edges of all the parts to remove any sharp edges, burrs and pencil marks. This photo shows a nicely rounded cat.*

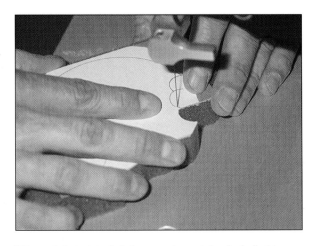

Photo 4:1 *A tight-holed sponge is used for the ball. Use spray adhesive to attach the pattern to the cardboard and then to the top of the sponge. Cut the sponge with a scroll saw.*

Photo 4:2 *Trim the sponge to a ball shape with scissors.*

Photo 4:3 *Sand the sponge to a smoothly rounded shape with a sander. For less firm sponges, use scissors.*

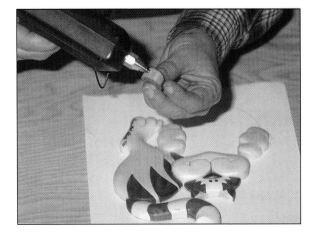

Photo 5:1 *Apply a clear finish to all the parts. Glue some of the stripes together. Here, I am gluing the tail section.*

Depending on the brand, you will only have seconds to adjust the parts before the glue sets up. You could use wood glue; it just takes a little longer to set up.

Photo 5:2

Here, I am gluing the parts together. This makes it a little easier to lay out the backing. I glued the tail section together, the stripes on the face, and the stripes on the back. You could glue the ears together, if desired. I sign the project after it has been finished, using a permanent marker. Signing the piece after it has been sealed prevents the ink from bleeding into the wood.

Photo 5:3

I trace around the actual project to get an outline for the backing rather than using the pattern. Sometimes in the sanding process, pieces may get altered or perhaps fit a little better with the head turned a little. Tracing around the actual project ensures that the backing will match the project exactly.

Note: If you are planning to mount the cat (or any Intarsia miniature) to something like a jewelry box, letter holder, or some other type of project, it is not necessary to make a backing. Just glue the pieces directly to the face of the project.

Remember to put the ball template in place and trace around it as well. I do my layout on a piece of paper. It helps to spray a very light coat of spray adhesive on the paper and then place the cat parts on top; it keeps the parts from sliding around while you trace the cat. Then apply the paper with spray adhesive to a 1/8" plywood board. I've found that Baltic birch works great.

Photo 5:4

After tracing completely around the cat, cut out the backing, stay to the inside of the pencil line. You will want the backing slightly smaller than the actual cat.

Photo 5:5

After de-burring the backing, I put a dark brown stain around the edges. I also applied the stain to the areas where the sponge ball joins the body. The dark circle will help to hide any areas on the sponge that were over-sanded. If you have any gaps in your project, stain the backing under the gap. I spray the backside of the backing with clear acrylic.

Photo 5:6

The cat is now ready to glue down to the backing. Place the parts on the backing and check all the edges to make sure there is no backing sticking out. If the backing is exposed, you will need to mark those areas and trim them on your saw. Once the edges of the backing are flush with the project, re-stain the edges.

Photo 5:7

Pick a few key parts to lock the project in place. The hind leg and tail section are good locking parts for this project. I put dots of wood glue, leaving space for a few dots of hot glue. Using two different types of glue is important. The hot glue sets quickly and works like a clamp. This will help anchor the project and keep the pieces from shifting as you continue.

Photo 5:8

Use a few dots of hot glue to work as a clamp. If you are using hot glue, you have to move fast and accurately before the glue sets up. Five to 10 seconds is all the time you'll have before the glue sets up.

Photo 5:9

Press the tail section down firmly and hold it

Photo 5:2 *Lay the pieces together on a piece of paper to be used for the backing pattern.*

Photo 5:3 *Trace around the cat to make an outline for the backing.*

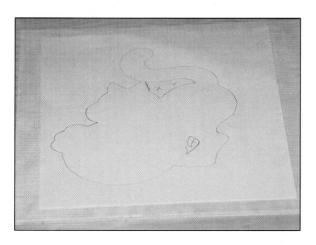

Photo 5:4 *Always trace the finished project. The cat's dimensions may have changed some from the original pattern. Cut out the backing, staying inside the lines.*

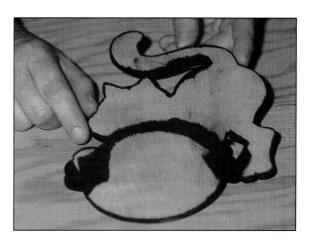

Photo 5:5 *Remove any burrs from the backing and stain the edges and around the outline of the ball.*

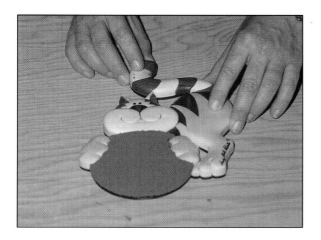

Photo 5:6 *Place the parts on the backing.*

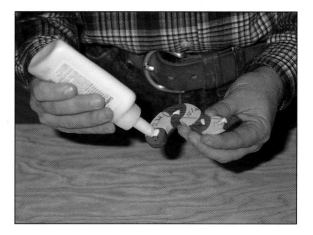

Photo 5:7 *Apply some wood glue to the back of the tail section. Leave space for a few drops of hot glue.*

in place for at least ten seconds. This will give the glue enough time to set up.

Photo 5:10

Use the same gluing technique on the hind leg section. Use some wood glue with a few dots of hot glue to act as a clamp and keep the other parts from shifting around during the gluing process.

Photo 5:11

Press firmly to keep the hind leg section in place until the hot glue sets up. For the rest of the project, I just use the wood glue as there is less pressure of getting the piece in the right place before the glue sets up. I use hot glue to glue the sponge in place. After the glue sets up use a hanger of your choice.

Small Intarsia Projects Buyers' Resources

Easy to Make Inlay Wood Projects -INTARSIA
Our first book that helped popularize Intarsia
Fox Chapel Publishing
PO Box 7948
Lancaster, PA 17604

Intarsia Times Newsletter (free)
Roberts Studio
Box 1925
Lufkin Texas 75902

Double Pneumatic Drum Sander
Sand-Rite Manufacturing Company
3221 North Justine St.
Chicago, IL 60607
312-997-2200

The following items are available from your local woodworking store or from many mail-order catalog companies.

Flex Drum Sander
Intarsia Detail Sander
Wonder Wheel
12" Aspen Wooden Plates
Bartley Wiping Gel (white or clear)
Bartley Wiping Gel (matte)
If you have difficulty locating any of the above please contact Roberts Studio at 1-800-316-09010 for details on ordering direct.

Photo 5:8 *Place a couple drops of hot glue, as well, on the back of the tail section.*

Photo 5:9 *Quickly, before the hot glue has a chance to set, glue the tail section on the backing.*

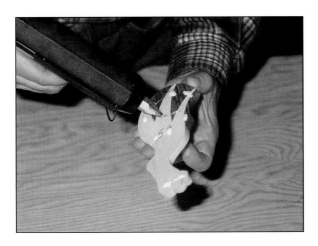

Photo 5:10 *Repeat the gluing process with the hind leg section.*

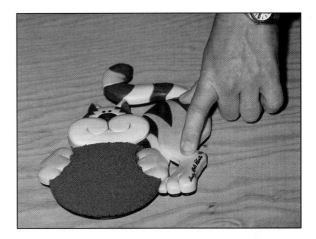

Photo 5:11 *Press firmly for 10 seconds until the hot glue sets up. Finish the project by using wood glue to on the rest of the wood pieces. Use hot glue on the sponge.*

LARGE MOUTH BASS

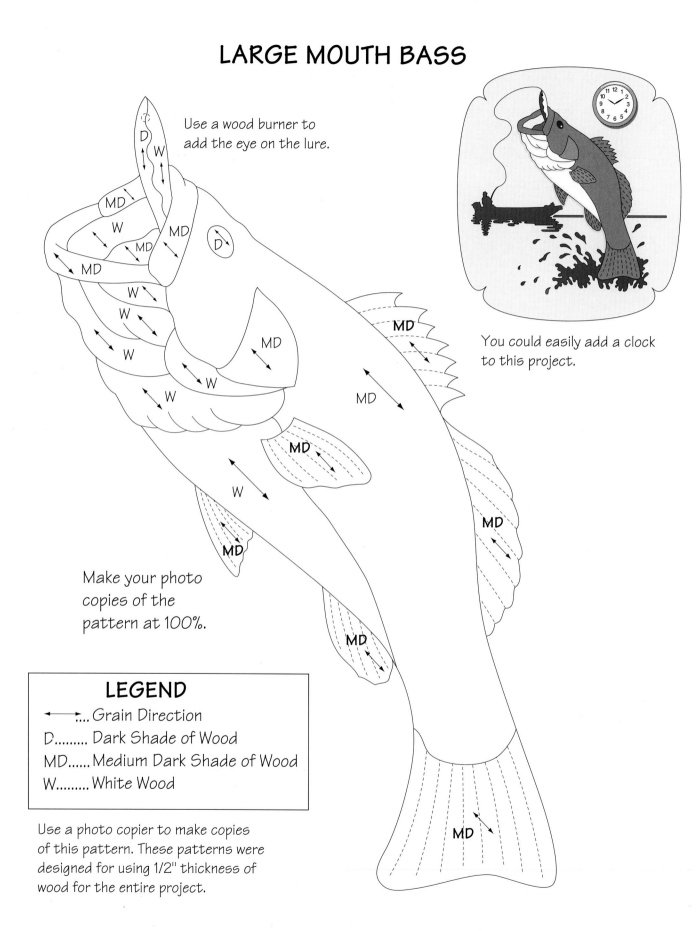

Use a wood burner to add the eye on the lure.

You could easily add a clock to this project.

Make your photo copies of the pattern at 100%.

LEGEND

→ ... Grain Direction
D .... Dark Shade of Wood
MD ...... Medium Dark Shade of Wood
W .... White Wood

Use a photo copier to make copies of this pattern. These patterns were designed for using 1/2" thickness of wood for the entire project.

For detailed instructions for making this project, read the chapter on the Large Mouth Bass.

Chapter Three
Large Mouth Bass

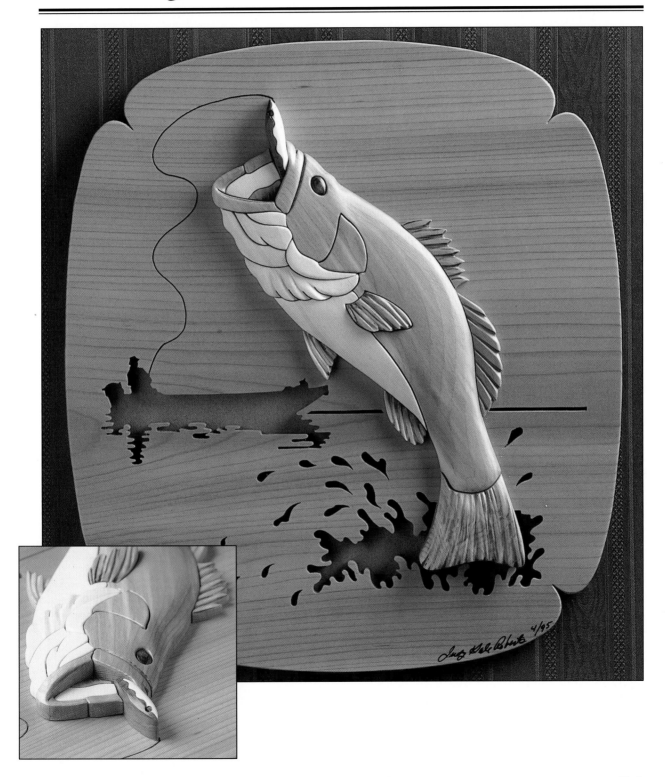

STEP ONE
LAYING OUT AND SAWING
THE BASS

Photo 1:1

You will need at least four copies of the pattern. Cut up the pattern and do the layout the same as for the cat in Chapter Two. I used ¹/₂" thick wood for the bass and the lure.

Photo 1:2

The entire bass can be stacked. The fins can be part of the stack or cut individually. The lure can be stacked also. I put the medium dark wood on top of the white wood when stacking wood for this project.

After the two colors have been taped together, I saw the fish. First, make sure that the burr has been removed from the back side of the bottom part. I made the first cut to the mouth section where the lure fits. After cutting the lure area, I then cut the outline, starting at the top of the head and moving down toward the back fins. However, it really doesn't make any difference which way you cut the outline.

When I got to the fins on the back, I chose to make a quick turn and follow along the outside of the fins, leaving them attached. As another option, you could follow the back of the fish leaving the fins attached to the drop off piece and then come back and saw them.

Follow the outline completely around the fish. I also chose to cut around the fins on the underside leaving them attached. After cutting the fish outline and removing the burr on the back, I then sawed off all four outside fins.

This completes the outside sawing of the fish. Careful planning must now be done before cutting the rest of the parts. The object at this point is to plan ahead, so you will be able to cut off each individual part from the

fish body. After cutting each part from the body, I turn the fish over and remove the burr. Once the body has been completely sawed, I then take apart the two larger stacked parts where the eye is located, making it single thickness. Drill the eye with a small drill, thread the blade through it, and saw out the eye hole. Finally, I sawed the lure and the eye piece.

Photo 1:3

After all the parts are cut out, check the fit and trim the wood where necessary.

STEP TWO
SHAPING THE BASS

Photo 2:1

The basic shape of the bass can be sanded as a unit. I made a sanding shim in the shape of the bass without the outer fins.

Photo 2:2

I am now ready to start shaping the bass. As with all Intarsia projects, you lower (or remove wood from) pieces to make the remaining pieces appear thicker. The lowered pieces are the parts that would be the farthest from the viewer. On the bass, the outer fins would be the farthest and, therefore, they should be sanded first. I lower the fins to a little less than ¹/₄". Then I use a pencil to mark where each fin joins the body.

Photo 2:3

When you are sanding the body, you do not want to sand lower than the fins. These pencil lines will be a guide for you to know when to stop sanding.

Photo 2:4

Now you are ready to sand the body. Put the body parts upside down. Take out the eye, the

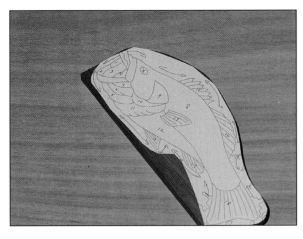

Photo 1:1 *Cut up and lay out the pattern following the procedures discussed in Chapter Two.*

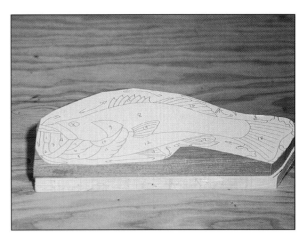

Photo 1:2 *Stack the two pieces of wood and hold them together with double-sided tape. Use spray adhesive to hold the pattern in place.*

Photo 1:3 *Start making cuts at the fish's mouth. In this photo, all the parts of the fish have been cut out*

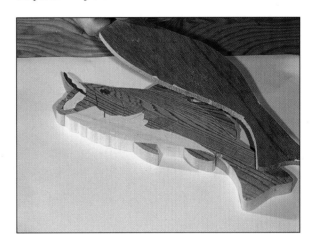

Photo 2:1 *Sand the bass as one unit. Cut a sanding shim to the shape of the bass and attach it to the back of the wood pieces.*

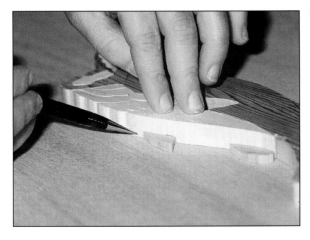

Photo 2:2 *The pieces farthest from the viewer should be the thinnest. Sand the fins to a little less than ¹/4″ and mark the height of each fin on the body.*

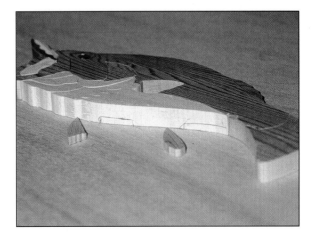

Photo 2:3 *Do not sand the body to a height lower than the fins.*

fin, and the gill portion cut in the medium dark wood. These parts need to be slightly thicker, so we do not want to sand them with the rest of the body parts. Put double-sided tape on the back of the bass parts.

Photo 2:5
Put the sanding shim in place, pressing the shim and the wood firmly together to make sure the tape sticks securely.

Photo 2:6
Sanding the bass as a unit is much faster than sanding the individual pieces and I want the fish's body to have a consistent shape. I have seen many projects that take on a quilted appearance because each piece has been rounded. Remember, a color change on the pattern does not mean a change in the overall shape of the subject.

Please note the pieces I did not tape on the backing—the eye, side fin and a part of the gill section. These parts will need to be thicker, therefore, they will be sanded individually.

Photo 2:7
Rough-in the body part of the bass; it is almost a torpedo shape. Remember to watch your pencil marks when rounding the sides.

Photo 2:8
I tapered the body down toward the base of the tail and up at the tip of the tail. This gives the bass a "flipping" tail and a more life-like appearance.

Photo 2:9
After I am satisfied with the basic shape of the bass, I take apart some of the gill section to sand the portions to give it a layered look. I use a small chisel to help remove the parts. Be careful not to dent any of the parts.

Photo 2:10
Next, I take out all the white parts of the gill section. I re-sand the lower body portion, tapering it toward the removed parts.

Photo 2:11
Put the next gill section in place and use a pencil to mark the freshly sanded area where it joins the next piece.

Photo 2:12
Sand this gill part, tapering it toward the mouth or the next un-sanded part. Mark this part where it joins the next piece.

Photo 2:13
Continue this process, tapering toward the next un-sanded part each time to give a stair-step pattern. I keep going until I reach the mouth.

Photo 2:14
Use a pencil to mark where the white sections join the mouth. Sand the mouth to follow the same contour as the white sections.

Photo 2:15
Sand the medium dark gill section so it is slightly thicker than the rest of that area.

Photo 2:16
The side fin would look better if it's thicker than the rest of the bass. The easiest way to do this is to raise that section. Trace around the fin on some 1/8" plywood.

Photo 2:17
Cut to the inside of the line, and glue this shim to the backside of the fin.

Photo 2:18
Put the raised fin where it belongs and mark

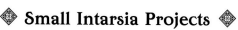

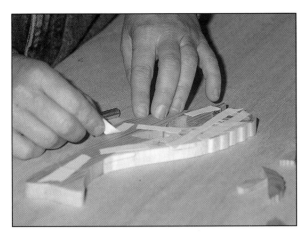

Photo 2:4 *Remove the eye, fin and gill sections and set them aside. They will be thicker than the rest of the body and sanded later.*

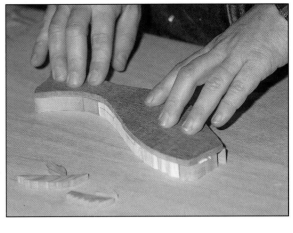

Photo 2:5 *With double-sided tape, attach the remaining pieces to the sanding shim.*

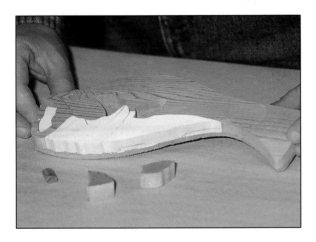

Photo 2:6 *Keep in mind that color changes do not mean a change in shape. The fish is streamlined and will be sanded as one unit.*

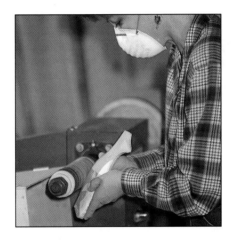

Photo 2:7 *Rough-in the body of the fish. Do not remove wood below the pencil marks you made to indicate the height of the fins.*

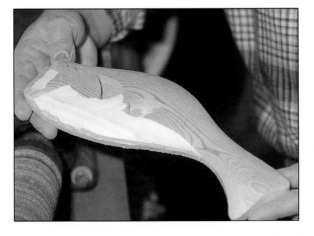

Photo 2:8 *Taper the body down at the base of the tail and up at the tip of the tail to add to the appearance of a flipping tail.*

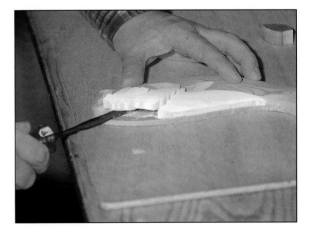

Photo 2:9 *Take apart the gill section. Use the sander and a chisel to give it a layered look.*

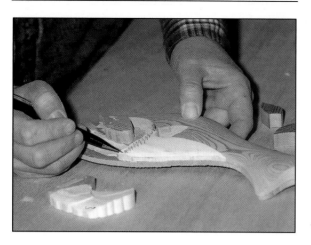

Photo 2:10 *Remove the white parts of the gill section and re-sand the lower body, tapering it toward the removed parts.*

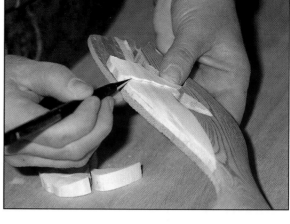

Photo 2:11 *Put the next gill section in place and use a pencil to mark the freshly sanded area where it joins the next piece.*

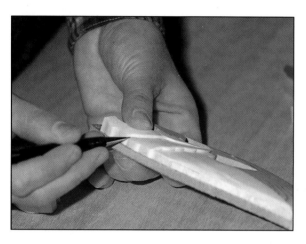

Photo 2:12 *Sand this gill part, tapering it toward the mouth or the next un-sanded part. Mark this part where it joins the next piece.*

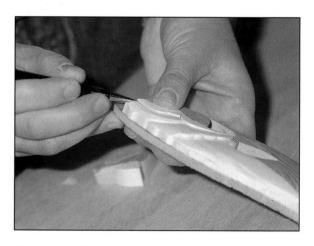

Photo 2:13 *Continue this process tapering toward the next un-sanded part each time to give a stair-step pattern, until you reach the mouth.*

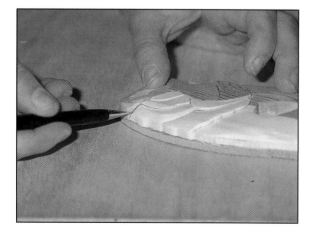

Photo 2:14 *Mark where the white sections join the mouth and sand the mouth to follow the same contour that the white sections follow.*

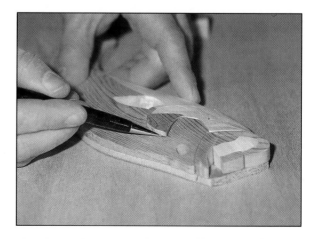

Photo 2:15 *Sand the medium dark gill section so it is slightly thicker than the rest of that area.*

Photo 2:16 *To make the side fin thicker than the rest of the bass, simply raise the side fin by putting a piece of ¹/8″ plywood under it and tracing the fin's outline.*

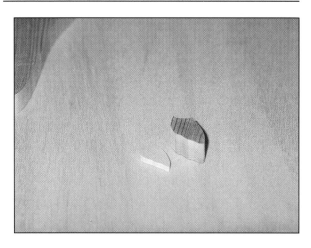

Photo 2:17 *Cut to the inside of the line and glue this piece to the back of the fin.*

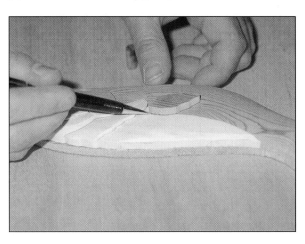

Photo 2:18 *Put the raised fin in place and mark its height with a pencil. When I sanded this fin, I tapered it down toward the bass's mouth, sanding down to the pencil line.*

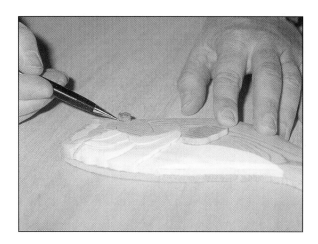

Photo 2:19 *Add the eye and use a pencil to mark where the body joins the eye. When you round the eye do not sand below this pencil line.*

Photo 2:20 *Round the eye with a sander and then burnish it with the Wonder Wheel.*

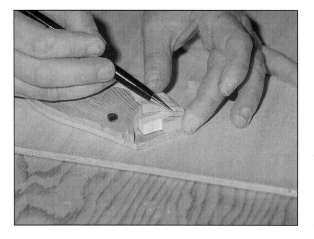

Photo 2:21 *Sand the inner mouth down toward the inside to give the mouth more depth.*

with pencil where the body joins the raised fin. When I sanded this fin, I tapered it down toward the bass's mouth, sanding down to the pencil line.

Photo 2:19

Put the eye in its place and mark where the body joins the eye. When you round the eye do not sand below this pencil line.

Photo 2:20

I rounded the eye with a sander, then went over the top of it with the Wonder Wheel. This burns the wood slightly (depending on how much pressure you use, you can control the burning) and burnishes it, giving it a sheen.

Photo 2:21

To give the mouth section more depth, I sanded the inner mouth part down toward the inside; the lowest side is about $1/8$".

Photo 2:22

I also sanded a dip on the upper lip section, as shown with the pencil shading.

Photo 2:23

Sand the mouth section, sanding off all the pencil marks on the upper lip section. Note the mouth now has much more depth.

Photo 2:24

Next mark the lure, indicating the thickness of the adjoining mouth parts. Taper the lure down toward the bass, sanding just below the upper mouth. Then slightly round the lure, watching those pencil lines on the sides. You want the lure to be thicker than the inside portion of the mouth.

Photo 2:25

Now, I am ready to do some detail work on the fins and some of the gill. Where the gills have been cut with the vein-type lines, I do a little carving. Again, I used the Wonder Wheel for this purpose, but a curved blade on a exacto knife will do the trick. I just carve it enough to give it some definition, almost another stair-step procedure.

Photo 2:26

Use a pencil to mark the lines on the fins, using the dashed lines on the pattern as a guide.

Photo 2:27

Mark the lines on the tail also.

Photo 2:28

On the fins and tail section, I used the edge of the Wonder Wheel to carve grooves. You can also use the edge of a disc sander to give the same effect. If using a disc sander, it is a good idea to trim around the sanding disc so it is not hanging over the metal backing. If you have none of the above equipment, a wood burner will work, just burn the areas indicated by the dashed line.

Photo 2:29

After shaping the lure, I glued the two parts together. Then with a wood burner, I burned a dot for the eye. The bass is just about complete at this time. Finish sand all the parts, sanding out any scratches or dings. Then sand around the edge of each piece removing the sharp corner and erase any remaining pencil lines.

Photo 2:30

When you are satisfied with the shaping, you are ready to work on the fretwork background section or, if desired, you can trace around the bass on some plywood to make a backing for a free-form bass, instead of the fretwork background.

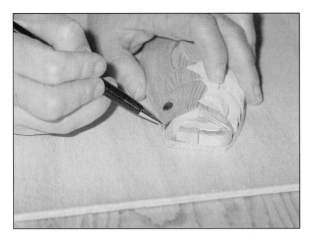

Photo 2:22 *Sand a dip on the upper lip. It is marked here in pencil.*

Photo 2:23 *Sand the mouth section. Make sure to sand off all the pencil marks on the upper lip. Note the mouth now has much more depth.*

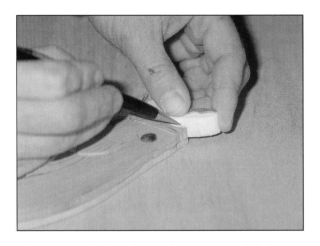

Photo 2:24 *Mark the lure and taper it toward the bass.*

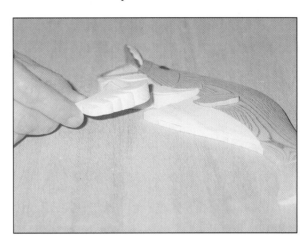

Photo 2:25 *Use a Wonder Wheel or exacto knife to add detail to the fin and the gills.*

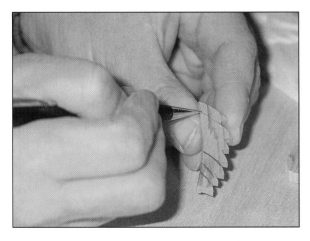

Photo 2:26 *Following the pattern, use a pencil to mark the lines on the fins.*

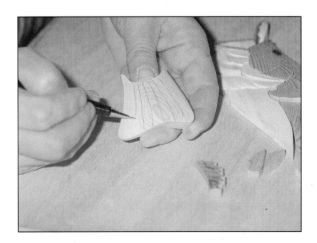

Photo 2:27 *Mark these lines on the tail as well.*

STEP THREE
FRETWORK AND BACKING

Photo 3:1

Put the finished bass on the pattern for the fretwork background. (The fretwork pattern appears on page 43.) Check to make sure it fits around the tail section; perhaps some of the tail was sanded off in the rounding process. You can mark the pattern and follow the new line when cutting out that section.

Photo 3:2

Also check the fishing line to make sure it lines up with the lure. If not, re-draw the line to match the lure. The pattern for the backing is now ready to be applied to the wood. I used cedar planed down to about 3/8". It would be good to use a color lighter than the medium dark part of the bass and darker than the white sections. In other words, a light piece of wood will work great.

Photo 3:3

After the sanding of the fish is completed and the layout has been done to the back plate, it is time to saw it. Drill all areas marked with an X.

Photo 3:4

Thread the blade through one of the drilled holes. I made all the inside fret cuts first and then sawed the outside of the plaque. I started with the tail section.

Photo 3:5

Continue cutting around the tail section.

Photo 3:6

Rather than leave this cut-out area one big part, you may want to cut across and remove a portion of the cut-out area.

Photo 3:7

After cutting the fretwork portion and around the outside edge, sand and de-burr the background of the bass project and use the finish of your choice. I used Bartley Wiping Gel (for more information on the gel see the Buyers Guide on page 28). Apply the finish to the fretwork background and to the bass.

I found it easier on this type project to glue the sections of the bass back together, side to side. I glued everything except the fins on the upper and lower part of the body.

Photo 3:8

You can glue the bass down at this time. I used the yellow woodworking glue; it is a good idea to have a damp paper towel handy for any oozing glue. Carefully line up the bass with the tail cut-out area and the fishing line for the lure to make sure it will line up correctly. Then lift it up and add some drops of glue. Do not flood the parts with glue; spread it evenly on the underside of the bass and glue it down. Then glue the fins down. I sign the project after the wood has been finished, using a permanent marker.

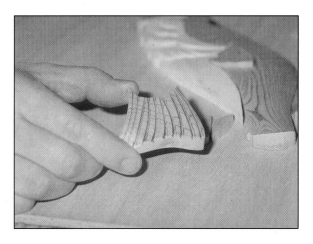

Photo 2:28 *Use a Wonder Wheel or a disc sander to carve the lines in the wood. A wood burner may also be used.*

Photo 2:29 *Burn a dot for the eye. Finish-sand the project, then lightly sand each piece to remove any pencil marks or sharp edges.*

Photo 2:30 *The finished fish.*

Photo 3:1 *Place the finished fish on the fretwork pattern, adjusting the pattern lines as necessary to fit the fish.*

Photo 3:2 *Adjust the fishing line to meet the lure.*

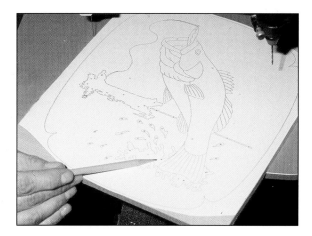

Photo 3:3 *Drill all the areas marked with an X.*

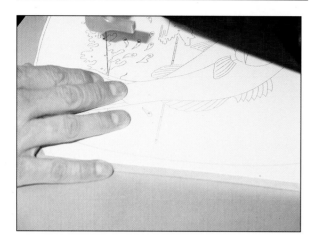

Photo 3:4 *Thread the blade through one of the drilled holes.*

Photo 3:5 *Continue cutting around the tail section.*

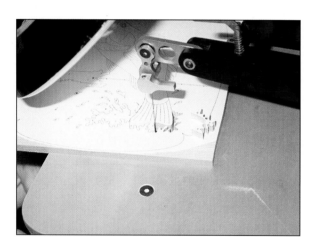

Photo 3:6 *Remove additional portions.*

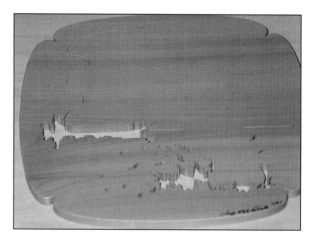

Photo 3:7 *Remove any burrs and rough edges from the fretwork background and stain it. Glue all the parts of the bass, except the fins, together.*

Photo 3:8 *Glue the bass to the background with yellow woodworking glue. Then glue on the fins.*

LARGE MOUTH BASS FRETWORK BACKGROUND

Enlarge this pattern 167%

All of the areas marked with an "x" are areas meant to be cut out. Drill into each section and thread your scroll saw blade into each drilled hole. We used a medium color piece of wood about 3/8" thick. Make an enlarged (167%) copy of the above pattern and spray adhesive on the back of the pattern, then apply the pattern to the wood.

For detailed instructions for making this project, read the chapter on the Large Mouth Bass. The intarsia bass (as pictured in the photo of the finished project) is on the previous page.

RACCOON

Pre-drill for the following dowels. You will need one 1/8" dowel for the eyes and one 1/4" dowel for the nose.

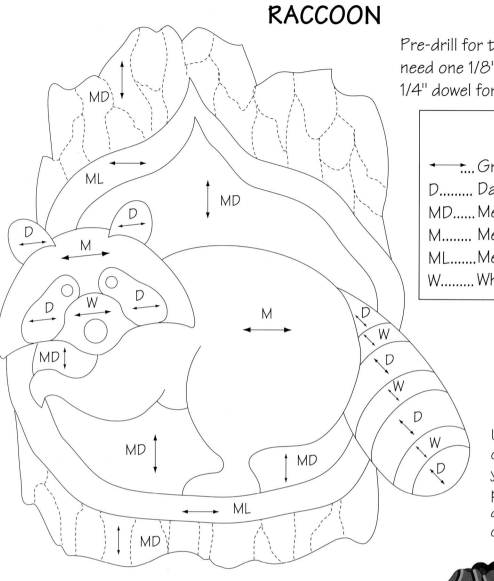

LEGEND

⟷ .... Grain Direction
D......... Dark Shade of Wood
MD...... Medium Dark Shade of Wood
M........ Medium Shade of Wood
ML....... Medium Light Shade of Wood
W........ White Wood

Make your photo copies of the pattern at 100%.

Use a photo copier to make copies of this pattern (if stack cutting, you will need at least seven copies per project). These patterns were designed for using 1/2" thickness of wood for the entire project.

Use a wood burner to add the "bark like" texture on the tree, using the dashed lines as a guide.

You could easily modify this pattern to make a napkin/letter holder.

Roberts Studio
P.O. Box 1925
Lufkin, Tx 75902

Chapter Four
Raccoon

Raccoon

Follow these techniques for the Raccoon, then make the other projects in this book using the techniques you have learned so far.

You will need a $1/4$" dowel for the nose and $1/8$" dowel for the eyes. Drill the parts before cutting them out.

Layout Tips: Make at least seven copies of the pattern. The tail section and the face can be stack-cut, if you want to attempt cutting three pieces at one time. I made the project with $1/2$" thick wood, so you would be cutting a total of $1 1/2$" with the three colors stacked. I stacked the dark and medium dark sections on the face and then cut the white part by itself. Stack cutting is not a must, you can lay out each piece on a single thickness of wood, if desired.

Sanding Tips: Remember to lower sections, starting at what would be the farthest from the viewer. On this project, the hole in the tree would be the thinnest. I sanded this area down to about $3/16$", then sanded the outer tree portion down to about $1/4$", rounding toward the outside edges. Marking adjoining pieces as you go with a pencil. Next, sand the light outline pieces that frame in the hole. Watch your pencil lines. You will want to keep these parts thicker than the tree part and the background in the hole section.

Make a sanding shim for the tail and for the face (trace around the assembled tail section and face section onto a piece of scrap plywood). Working our way up to the thicker parts, the next section will be the tail. Use some double-sided tape to stick the tail on the sanding shim. I tapered the tail down towards the body, then rounded the outside edges. Watch your pencil lines where the tree touches the tail. You do not want to sand the tail lower than the tree. Mark where the tail joins the body and sand the body, lowering the area around the face to make the face appear thicker. Mark the head where it joins the body. Next sand the ears. I tapered the ears down toward the head. Mark where they join the head. Put the head on a sanding shim using double-sided tape. Note all the pencil lines showing the height of adjoining pieces. You do not want to sand below any of these lines. If you do happen to sand off a little too much, don't worry — you can re-sand adjoining parts.

For the eyes I used a $1/8$" dowel. I cut a section about $1 1/2$" long and slightly rounded both ends. I used the Wonder Wheel, which burns and rounds the dowel at the same time. You could round the eyes and use a wood burner or stain to darken the eyes. If you can locate $1/8$" walnut dowel, there will be no need to darken it for the eyes. I then put the dowel in the pre-drilled hole for the eye and mark the dowel from the backside of the head. I like to have the eyes almost flush with the head to keep the raccoon from looking bug eyed. After both dowels are cut I glue them in. I used a $1/4$" walnut dowel for the nose. I cut the dowel so it would stick out about $1/16$" from the nose.

The final sanding step is to lightly sand the edge of all the parts to knock off the sharp corner and erase any remaining pencil marks. Now it is time to put a finish on.

Detailing Tips: To add extra detail to the project I used a wood burner to give the tree a "bark-like" texture. I used two different tips: one to burn the bark lines and the other tip to do shading which gives the bark more depth.

This design would make a great napkin/letter holder, for details on making a napkin holder look at the dolphin project.

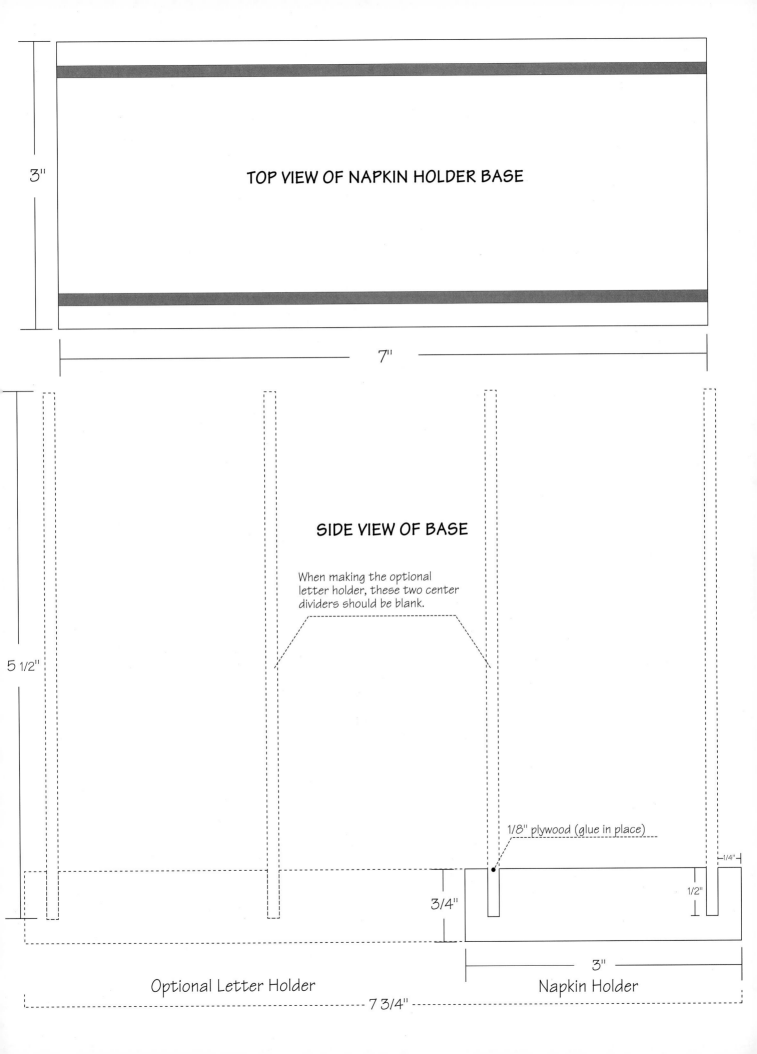

TOP VIEW OF NAPKIN HOLDER BASE

3"

7"

SIDE VIEW OF BASE

When making the optional letter holder, these two center dividers should be blank.

5 1/2"

1/8" plywood (glue in place)

1/4"

3/4"

1/2"

3"

Optional Letter Holder

Napkin Holder

7 3/4"

Wren

Make your photo copies of
the pattern at 100%.
These patterns were designed
for using 1/2" thickness of wood
for the entire project.

Pre-drill for the following dowel: You will
need one 1/8" dowel for the eye.

LEGEND

←——→... Grain Direction
D......... Dark Shade of Wood
MD...... Medium Dark Shade of Wood
W........ White Wood

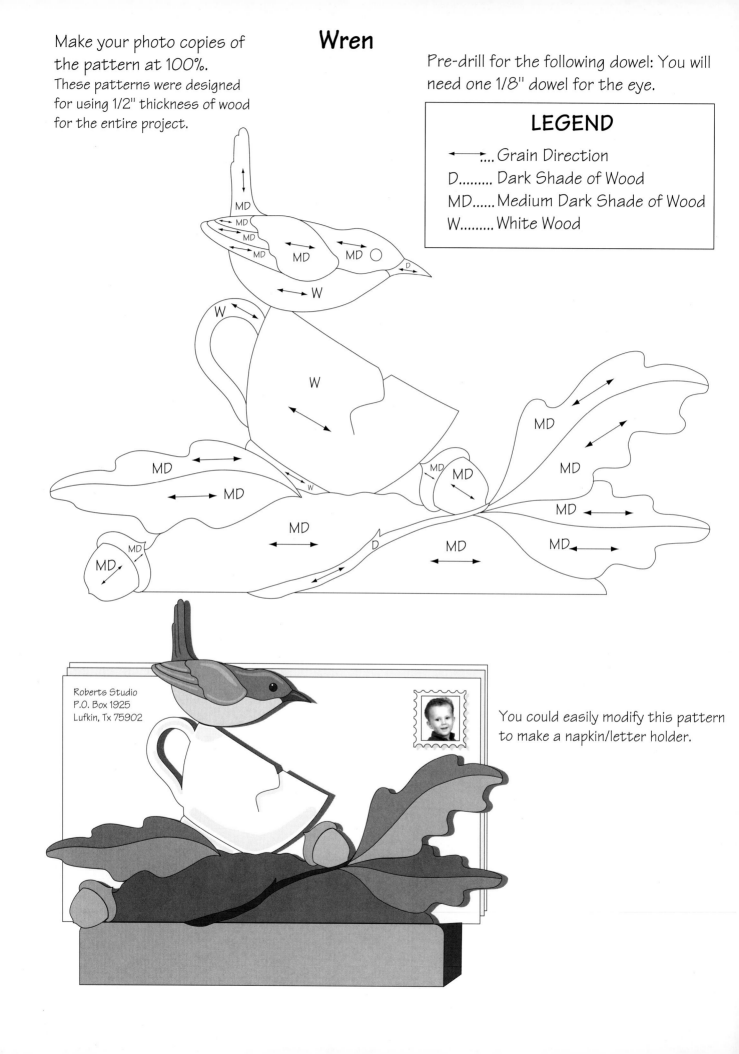

Roberts Studio
P.O. Box 1925
Lufkin, Tx 75902

You could easily modify this pattern
to make a napkin/letter holder.

Chapter Five
Wren

This wren would look great applied to a jewelry box. You can add some extra detail by using a wood burner to add texture to the acorn tops. I used a very light piece of basswood for the tea cup.

HUMMING BIRD

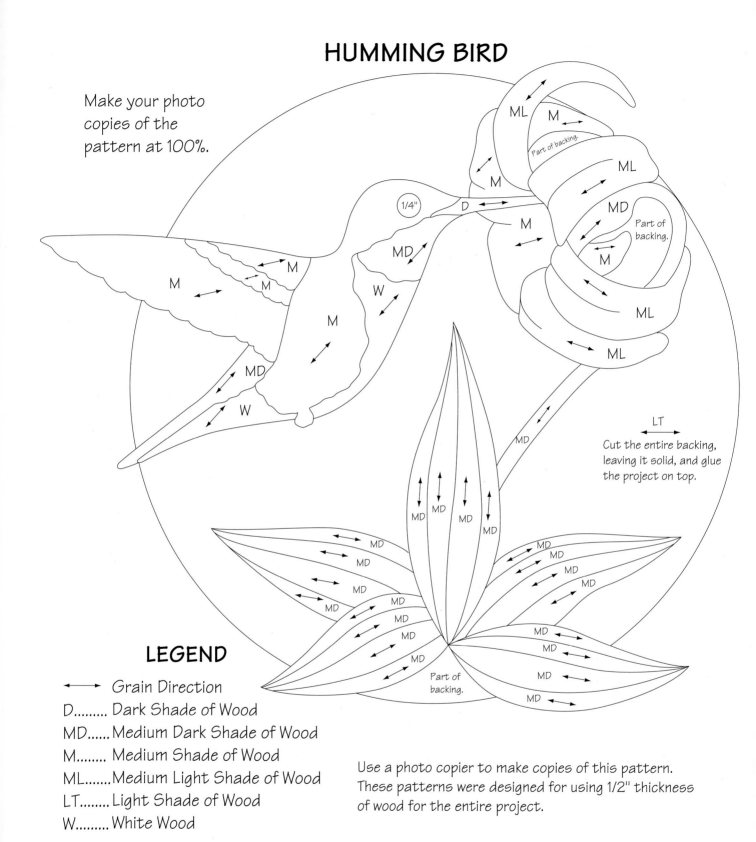

Make your photo copies of the pattern at 100%.

ML M

Part of backing.

ML

M

MD

Part of backing.

1/4"

D

M

M

MD

W

M

M

M

MD

W

M

M

MD

ML

ML

ML

LT

Cut the entire backing, leaving it solid, and glue the project on top.

MD

MD MD MD MD

MD

MD

MD

MD MD

MD MD MD

MD

MD

MD

MD

MD

MD

MD

MD

Part of backing.

LEGEND

⟷   Grain Direction

D......... Dark Shade of Wood

MD...... Medium Dark Shade of Wood

M........ Medium Shade of Wood

ML....... Medium Light Shade of Wood

LT........ Light Shade of Wood

W......... White Wood

Use a photo copier to make copies of this pattern. These patterns were designed for using 1/2" thickness of wood for the entire project.

Cut a 6 1/2" diameter circle for the backgroud. The humming bird and flower were glued on top. The leaves were cut into sections, however, you can leave them solid and burn the lines or leave them out all together. Drill 1/4" hole for the eye. I used a 1/4" walnut dowel to make the eye; you can use a regular dowel and stain or burn the end.

Chapter Six
Hummingbird

Wood that is light on the face of the board and dark on the back work great for petals. When you sand down into the wood, the dark portion is exposed and adds extra depth. You can use a woodburner on the leaves instead of cutting the lines.

BALD EAGLE

Use a wood burner to add a pupil to the eagle's eye, using the dashed lines as a guide.

You can add a round frame as shown with the dashed lines on the pattern.

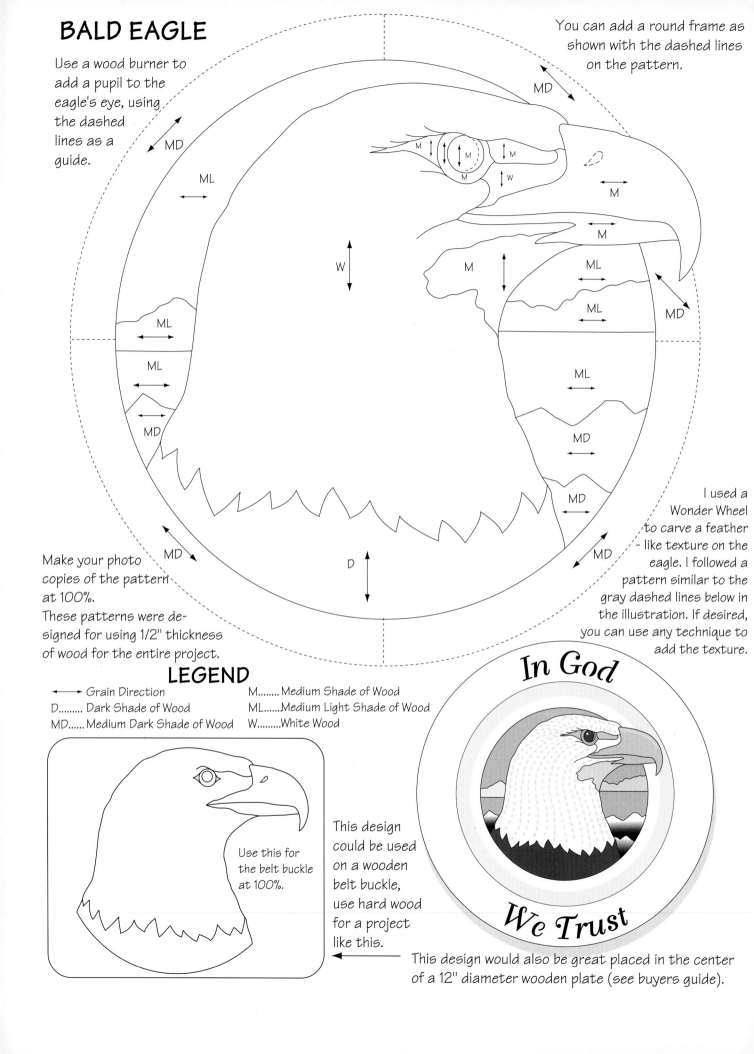

MD

MD

ML

M ↕ M ↕ M

M ↕ W

M

W

M

M

M

M

ML

ML

MD

ML

ML

ML

MD

MD

MD

MD

MD

D

Make your photo copies of the pattern at 100%.
These patterns were designed for using 1/2" thickness of wood for the entire project.

I used a Wonder Wheel to carve a feather-like texture on the eagle. I followed a pattern similar to the gray dashed lines below in the illustration. If desired, you can use any technique to add the texture.

LEGEND

←——→ Grain Direction
D......... Dark Shade of Wood
MD...... Medium Dark Shade of Wood

M........ Medium Shade of Wood
ML......Medium Light Shade of Wood
W.........White Wood

Use this for the belt buckle at 100%.

This design could be used on a wooden belt buckle, use hard wood for a project like this.

In God

We Trust

This design would also be great placed in the center of a 12" diameter wooden plate (see buyers guide).

Chapter Seven
Bald Eagle

You can stack-cut portions of this project. The white head with the beak and eye area are good candidates for stack-cutting. I used a Wonder Wheel to add a feather-like texture to the white portion of the head.

ROSE WITH BUDS

Use a photo copier to make copies of this pattern. These patterns were designed for using 1/2" thickness of wood for the entire project.

Make your photo copies of the pattern at 100%.

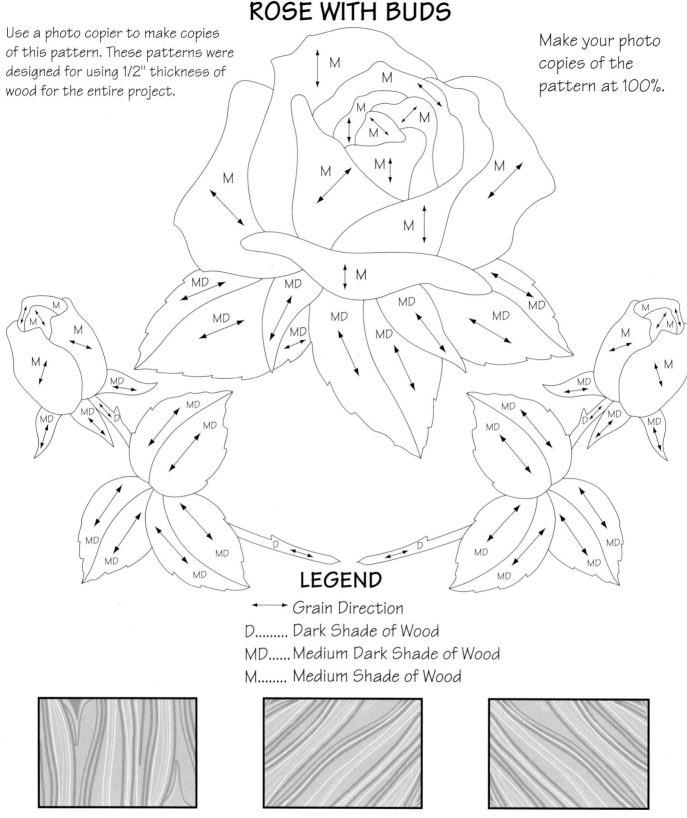

LEGEND

→ Grain Direction

D......... Dark Shade of Wood

MD...... Medium Dark Shade of Wood

M........ Medium Shade of Wood

The rose was designed to be stacked cut using three layers of medium color wood. Changing the grain directions, one will be vertical and the other two diagonal. After the parts are cut out swap the parts to have the grain directions going similar to the pattern. I found some wood with different color streaks running throughout the board, even using some boards a medium color to a almost white (sap wood). Use this technique for the petals only. the leaves and steams can be layed out individually.

This project looks great on a jewelry box, as shown in the photo. It would also look great in the center of a 12" diameter wooden plate, or free-form projects.

Chapter Eight
Rose with Buds

The rose is a fun project to shape. You can experiment with the petals.
The only rule to follow on most of the petals is to taper them in toward the next
petal. You can roll the outer edge, leave it sharp, or angle it toward the outer
edge. The more tapering toward the inner petals you do, the more dimensional
the flower will look. After the project was shaped and the finish was applied, I
glued the parts together (edge to edge) then glued it on top of the jewelry box. If
you have some pink, red or streaked wood, here is your chance to use it. Also, a
yellow rose would look wonderful.

DOLPHIN

"Common Dolphin"
Sometimes called the crisscross dolphin
because of the crisscross pattern on the sides.

LEGEND

←——→...Grain Direction
D.........Dark Shade of Wood
MD......Medium Dark Shade of Wood
M........Medium Shade of Wood
W........White Wood

Make your photo copies of the pattern at 100%. These patterns were designed for using 1/2" thickness of wood for the entire project.

Use a wood burner for the eye and if you want to put a smile on your dolphin, use the dashed lines as a guide.

The dolphin would look great in groups, you can stack the different colors and make sets going left and right. These work out well for refrigerator magnets or use on a jewelry box top, letter/napkin holder, or even free-form wall hangings.

Chapter Nine
Dolphin

You can stack the three colors involved in making the dolphin, however, only one will have the "correct" markings for a common dolphin. The other two will still look great. The pattern for a letter/napkin holder appears on page 47.

CHICKADEE

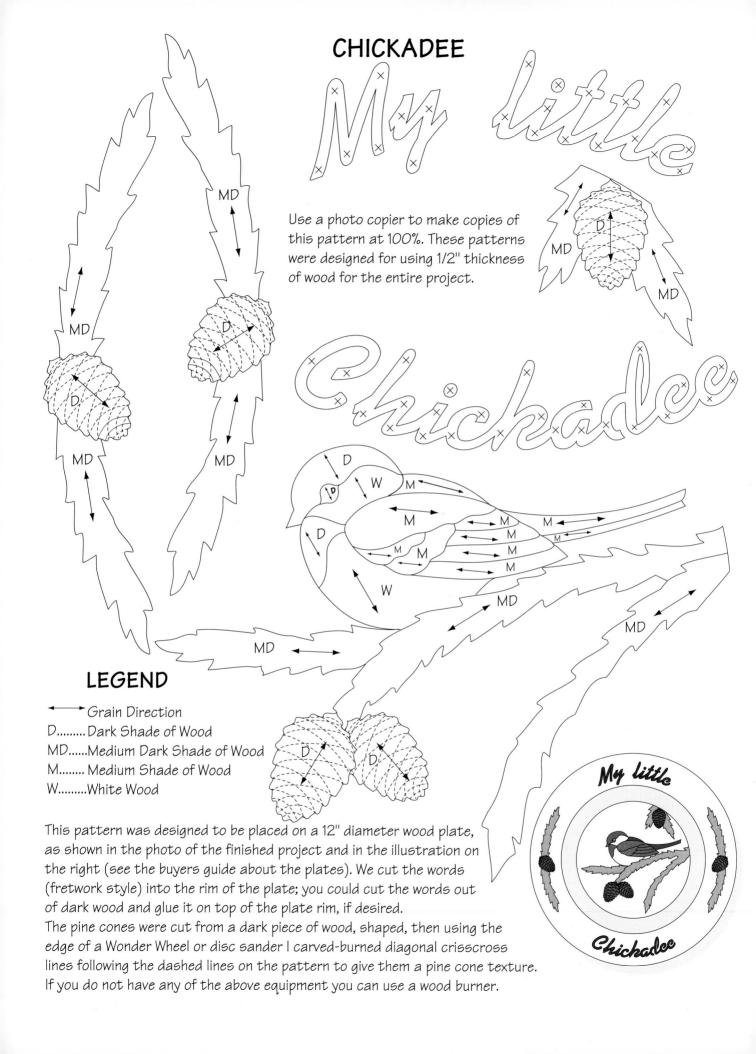

Use a photo copier to make copies of this pattern at 100%. These patterns were designed for using 1/2" thickness of wood for the entire project.

LEGEND

→ Grain Direction
D.........Dark Shade of Wood
MD......Medium Dark Shade of Wood
M........Medium Shade of Wood
W.........White Wood

This pattern was designed to be placed on a 12" diameter wood plate, as shown in the photo of the finished project and in the illustration on the right (see the buyers guide about the plates). We cut the words (fretwork style) into the rim of the plate; you could cut the words out of dark wood and glue it on top of the plate rim, if desired.
The pine cones were cut from a dark piece of wood, shaped, then using the edge of a Wonder Wheel or disc sander I carved-burned diagonal crisscross lines following the dashed lines on the pattern to give them a pine cone texture.
If you do not have any of the above equipment you can use a wood burner.

Chapter Ten
Chickadee

To help give a feather effect, I layered the wing feathers for greater definition. You can use the edge of a disc sander or a Wonder Wheel to carve the lines in the pine cones and on the pine branches.

Chapter Ten
Four Seasons

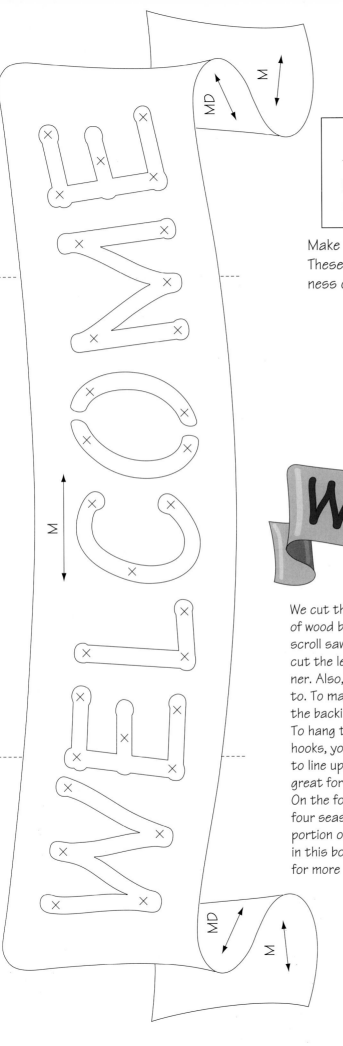

WELCOME BANNER
for the Seasons

Make your photo copies of the pattern at 100%. These patterns were designed for using 1/2" thickness of wood for the entire project.

We cut the word welcome out of the medium shade of wood by drilling in each letter and threading the scroll saw blade through the drilled hole. You could cut the letters out and glue them on top of the banner. Also, we made a 1/8" backing to glue all the parts to. To make the word "Welcome" stand out I stained the backing where the cut out sections show through. To hang the project we used some screw eyes and hooks, you can use the dashed lines on the pattern to line up the hooks. Some macrame string works great for hanging up the project.

On the following pages there are four plaques (the four seasons) designed to hang from the "Welcome" portion of this project. Many of the other designs in this book could be placed on the same size plaque for more of a variety.

WINTER SEASON

Cut the entire backing, leaving it solid, and glue the project on top.

ENLARGE THIS PATTERN 125%

LEGEND

←——→ .... Grain Direction
D .... Dark Shade of Wood
M .... Medium Shade of Wood
W .... White Wood

These patterns were designed for using 1/2" thickness of wood for the entire project. Use the outline of the project as a pattern for the background area. I cut out four (for each season plaque) using a medium light shade of wood about 3/8" to 1/2" thick, then glued the intarsia project on top of it.

Pre-drill for the following dowels. I used two 3/8" dowels for cheeks. After cutting the smile, I put the dowels in place and marked a continuation of the smile into the dowel. The nose is 3/16" and the two eyes are 1/8".

We finished the pieces individually, including the backing, then glued the intarsia project on top of the backing. If you plan to hang this from the "Welcome" banner, there are dashed lines above on the pattern to help you line up the hooks. You could make another smaller plaque to hang under this portion with your last name cut into it.

SPRING SEASON

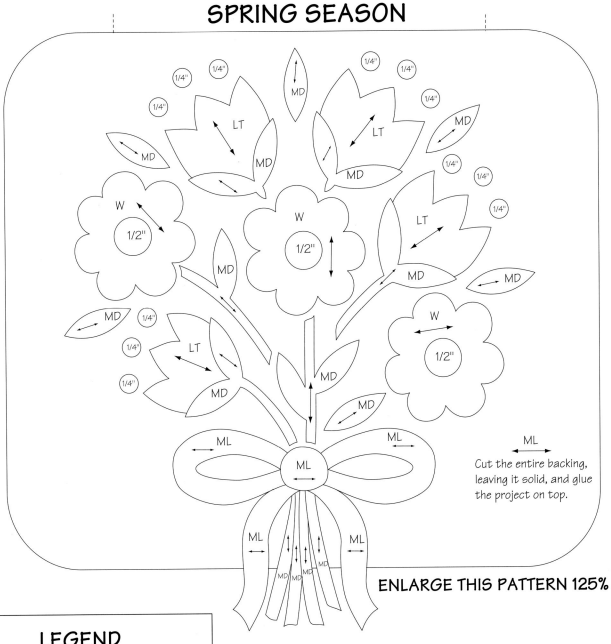

ENLARGE THIS PATTERN 125%

Cut the entire backing, leaving it solid, and glue the project on top.

LEGEND

→ Grain Direction
D......... Dark Shade of Wood
MD...... Medium Dark Shade of Wood
ML....... Medium Light Shade of Wood
LT....... Light Shade of Wood
W......... White Wood

These patterns were designed for using 1/2" thickness of wood for the entire project. Use the outline of the project as a pattern for the background area. I cut out four (for each season plaque) using a medium light shade of wood about 3/8" to 1/2" thick, then glued the intarsia project on top of it.

I used 1/2" walnut dowels for the flower centers, and 1/4" walnut dowels (cut about 1/4" long) glued in groups of threes above each tulip. If you do not have walnut dowels, you can stain the 1/4" dowels, and perhaps cut the 1/2" centers out of dark wood. We finished the pieces individually, including the backing, then glued the intarsia project on top of the backing. If you plan to hang this from the "Welcome" banner, there are dashed lines above on the pattern to help you line up the hooks. You could make another smaller plaque to hang under this portion with your last name cut into it. I am showing two colors for the flowers, after completeing the project I think it would look good with more of a variety of colors for the flowers.

SUMMER SEASON

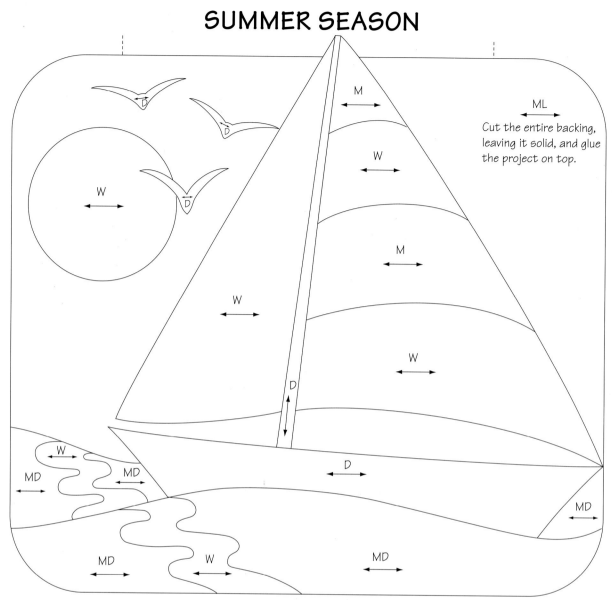

ENLARGE THIS PATTERN 125%

LEGEND

←——→ Grain Direction
D......... Dark Shade of Wood
MD.......Medium Dark Shade of Wood
M........ Medium Shade of Wood
W........ White Wood

These patterns were designed for using 1/2" thickness of wood for the entire project. Use the outline of the project as a pattern for the background area. I cut out four (for each season plaque) using a medium light shade of wood about 3/8" to 1/2" thick, then glued the intarsia project on top of it.

This project is ideal for stack cutting (stacking two or more colors of wood then swaping the parts). Especially on the striped sail and the water. When sanding the sail and the water, it will help to make a sanding shim (as explained in detail when making the "Pin Cushion Cat" and the "Bass").

We finished the pieces individually, including the backing, then glued the intarsia project on top of the backing. If you plan to hang this from the "Welcome" banner, there are dashed lines above on the pattern to help you line up the hooks. You could make another smaller plaque to hang under this portion with your last name cut into it.

FALL SEASON

ML — Cut the entire backing, leaving it solid, and glue the project on top.

ENLARGE THIS PATTERN 125%

Pre-drill for the following dowel: Use a 1/4" dowel for the eye and use a wood burner to add the corners on the eye (dashed lines) and the wisker detail on the mouse.

LEGEND

⟷ Grain Direction
D......... Dark Shade of Wood
MD...... Medium Dark Shade of Wood
M........ Medium Shade of Wood

These patterns were designed for using 1/2" thickness of wood for the entire project. Use the outline of the project as a pattern for the background area. I cut out four (for each season plaque) using a medium light shade of wood about 3/8" to 1/2" thick, then glued the intarsia project on top of it.

You can use up some of your scrap wood on this one, try to find some autumn colors (reds, golds, etc.) The leaves can be cut into individual pieces or use a wood burner to put the vein lines. We finished the pieces individually, including the backing, then glued the intarsia project on top of the backing. If you plan to hang this from the "Welcome" banner, there are dashed lines above on the pattern to help you line up the hooks. You could make another smaller plaque to hang under this portion with your last name cut into it.

INTARSIA PATTERNS available from JUDY GALE ROBERTS • Roberts Studio

P.O. BOX 1925 • LUFKIN, TX 75902 • 1 (800) 316-9010 • (409) 632-9663 • FAX (409) 632-7977

FOR A MORE DETAILED DESCRIPTION WITH PICTURES OF THE FOLLOWING PATTERNS,
PLEASE WRITE OR CALL THE ABOVE ADDRESS AND ASK FOR A COPY OF THE "INTARSIA TIMES".

PANDA	POLAR BEAR "ENDANGERED SPECIES SERIES"	STILL POTTERY
TOUCAN	TIGER "ENDANGERED SPECIES SERIES"	WOLF
RACCOON	ELEPHANT "ENDANGERED SPECIES SERIES"	OL' BLUE
CAT IN BAG	BLACK RHINO "ENDANGERED SPECIES SERIES"	FAWN AND DOE
SEASCAPE	SANTA	WHITE TAIL DEER
ROSE	WREATH	CHRISTMAS SIGN
CAT WITH YARN	DOLPHIN	ANGEL
KOALA BEARS	PENGUINS	ASIAN LION
BIG FOOT CLOWN	DOG	BARN
CLOWN IN WINDOW	U S A EAGLE	GOLFER
CLOWN WITH DAISIES	COW	BATTER UP
BUCK DEER	BEARS	CASTLE
HORSE	SWAN	ROOSTER WEATHER VEIN
BUTTERFLY AND ORCA	SAIL BOAT	BALD EAGLE
OH HOOT WEST	ARIZONA	ELK
MOUSE	UP CARROUSEL	HUMMING BIRD
CHRISTMAS STOCKINGS	DOWN CARROUSEL	COVERED BRIDGE
PELICAN	CAMEL	CHRISTMAS STOCKINGS #2
HOBO CLOWN	ROSE BUD	CARDINALS
FLAMINGOS	BARN OWL	WOMAN GOLFER
STILL LIFE	WABBIT	FRUIT STILL LIFE
LIGHT HOUSE	TROPICAL FISH	COWBOY
BALLOON	ANTIQUE SANTA	PUP WITH DECOY
DUCK	CHRISTMAS ORNAMENTS	RING NECK PHEASANT
PIG IN A BLANKET	OH HOOT HAWAIIAN	RED FOX
BAG LADY	ROCKY TOP	SNOWMAN AND CHICKADEE
CURIOUS COON	CALLAS FLOWER	NOAH'S ARK
BASS	FLORIDA PANTHER	SUN FLOWER WELCOME
CAT IN A CHAIR	MOOSE	CAT ON SHELF
BOG BUDDIES	GIRAFFE	FOOTBALL PLAYER
MANATEE "ENDANGERED SPECIES SERIES"	COYOTE	WOOD DUCK
		GERMAN SHEPHERD

**THE PATTERNS ABOVE ARE PRINTED FULL SIZE ON 17 1/2" x 23" TRANSPARENT TRACING PAPER,
EACH PATTERN COMES WITH A 8" x 10" BLACK AND WHITE PRINT OF THE FINISHED PROJECT.
THE PATTERNS ABOVE SELL FOR $6.95 EACH OR 3 FOR $18.95 PLUS $2.75 SHIPPING**

EAGLE	WOODLAND TRAIL	SEA GULL PILING	INDIAN WOMAN
CLOUD NINE	EAGLE LANDING	BUFFALO	MACAW PARADISE
LAST SUPPER	INDIAN	ON A LIMB COON	ALLIGATOR DREAMS
	OWL		

**THE PATTERNS ABOVE ARE PRINTED FULL SIZE ON 25" x 38" TRANSPARENT TRACING PAPER,
EACH PATTERN COMES WITH A 8" x 10" BLACK AND WHITE PRINT OF THE FINISHED PROJECT.
THE LARGER SIZE PATTERNS ABOVE SELL FOR $7.95 EACH OR 3 FOR $21.95**

Buy one or all of the patterns available for just one shipping charge of $2.75.

ALSO AVAILABLE;

TWO POSTER PATTERN SETS, "THE HIDDEN FOREST' AND "NEW SHOES" EACH SET COMES WITH A PATTERN
AND A 19" x 25 " FULL COLOR POSTER SUITABLE FOR FRAMING. $24.95 EACH PLUS 2.75 SHIPPING.
"FAMILY AFFAIR" COMES WITH 13" X 19" COLOR POSTER AND THE FINISHED FRAME SIZE IS 32.5" X 38". $19.95
EACH PLUS 2.75 SHIPPING.

A 90 MINUTE INTARSIA INSTRUCTIONAL VIDEO WHICH COVERS A BEGINNER LEVEL PATTERN FROM START TO
FINISH. $32.95

THE "FINE LINE DESIGN" BOOK SERIES
SCROLL SAW • FRETWORK PATTERN BOOKS *BY JUDY GALE ROBERTS*

The "Fine Line Design" is an original idea developed by professional artist Judy Gale Roberts and craftsman Jerry Booher.

These new designs are drawn with a line so thin, that when using a #1 scroll saw blade the line will be completely removed. By using the new "Fine Line" patterns, you will be able to better control the drift error found with thick line drawings (just drifting from one side of a thick line to the other will cause problems with the overall accuracy of a design).

Especially designed for the scroll saw enthusiast who wishes to excel at their hobby or profession. This eye-catching collection of new designs offers the working crafts-person or artist timesaving, professionally executed, ready to use patterns.

The lion above is a sample pattern (missing the outer train car frame) from Design Book #7 "Circus and Clowns". The areas marked with a "X" are cut out.

FINE LINE DESIGN BOOKS AVAILABLE

DESIGN BOOK #1
A GENERAL SUBJECT BOOK OF PATTERNS, FROM COWS TO PELICANS. $14.95

DESIGN BOOK #2
"WESTERN AND SOUTHWESTERN" PATTERNS OF COWBOYS, INDIANS, AND EVERY-THING IN BETWEEN. $16.95

DESIGN BOOK #3
"THE GREAT OUTDOORS" PATTERNS OF OUTDOOR SCENES FROM FISHING TO HOT AIR BALLOONS. $14.95

DESIGN BOOK #4
"SPORTS" PATTERNS, FROM BASEBALL TO FOOTBALL. $14.95

DESIGN BOOK #5
"HEARTLAND" PATTERNS OF RURAL AMERICA, INCLUDING FARMS TO BARNS. $14.95

DESIGN BOOK #6
"PETS AND PEOPLE" PATTERNS OF CATS TO DOGS AND MANY OTHER PETS. $14.95

DESIGN BOOK #7
"CIRCUS AND CLOWNS" PATTERNS OF CLOWNS, CIRCUS ANIMALS AND A WONDERFUL CIRCUS TRAIN. $14.95

Buy one or all seven books from Roberts Studio for just one shipping charge of $3.00